# A TREASURY OF
# Scrap Quilts

### NANCY J. MARTIN

*Martingale*®
& COMPANY

A Treasury of Scrap Quilts
© 2005 by Nancy J. Martin

That Patchwork Place® is an imprint of
Martingale & Company®.

Martingale & Company
20205 144th Avenue NE
Woodinville, WA 98072-8478 USA

## Credits

President • Nancy J. Martin
CEO • Daniel J. Martin
VP and General Manager • Tom Wierzbicki
Publisher • Jane Hamada
Editorial Director • Mary V. Green
Managing Editor • Tina Cook
Technical Editor • Laurie Baker
Copy Editor • Melissa Bryan
Design Director • Stan Green
Illustrator • Laurel Strand
Cover and Text Designer • Shelly Garrison
Photographer • Brent Kane

Printed in the U.S.A.

ISBN 1-56477-603-4

# Acknowledgments

Many thanks to the following people:

Millicent Agnor for her Amish quilting service and the women who work with her, especially Edna Borntreijor, Susie Hostetler, Elsie Mast, Treva Mast, Emma Miller, Fannie Mae Petersheim, Rose Schwartz, Anna Stutzman, Lydia Troyer, Clara Yoder, Fannie Yoder, and Anna Raber, who marks all the quilts for quilting;

Donna Gundlach, Sue von Jentzen, Hazel Montague, Alvina Nelson, and Fannie Schwartz for their fine hand quilting;

Julie Stewart for the use of "Keep the Shiny Side Up";

Mary Hickey for the use of "Overcoming Our Troubles";

Cleo Nollette for help in piecing and binding;

Terry Louise Martin for manuscript entry;

The Monday Night Bowling League for inspiration and encouragement.

# Contents

# Introduction

I made my first quilt in 1976, and so began a lifelong passion for scrap quilts. The quilt, a queen-size Log Cabin design, featured myriad brown and cream prints, which were not easy to find in 1976. Quilting was just becoming popular and fabric stores had not yet caught up with the trend. Quilt shops were virtually nonexistent. Thus, looking for 100%-cotton options in a particular color range among the polyester fabrics was a real challenge.

The look I envisioned for this first quilt had to utilize lots of different fabrics. As I fussed about the lack of cotton fabrics available for sewing, I remembered that 100% cotton was still used in ready-to-wear garments, especially men's shirts. Instantly I was off to my husband's closet with a pair of scissors in hand! My quilt vision became a reality as planned, and several long-sleeved shirts in various shades of brown and cream were fashioned into short-sleeved styles.

Making that first quilt was such a pleasurable experience for me that I couldn't wait to do another. The next one was also a Log Cabin scrap quilt, this time in blue.

Again the quilt began with trips to the fabric store and to my husband's closet. All of the quilts that I have made since have been multiple-fabric quilts.

The term "scrap quilt" suggests that one use leftover pieces, or scraps, of fabric. However, I have never made a quilt using fabrics just from my scraps. There is always the desire to go purchase more fabrics that will enhance those scraps. So, whether you're working from your scrap bag or purchasing all new fabrics to make a scrappy-looking quilt, remember my motto: "Why use 2 fabrics when you can use 20?"

# Making Scrap Quilts

I've learned a lot along the way about saving, sorting, and using my scraps that I'd like to share with you.

## SAVING SCRAPS

As a novice quilter with a small fabric stash, I used to save every single scrap of leftover fabric. Now, almost 30 years later, I have become more discerning about what scraps I save. Anything smaller than a 4" x 4" square is tossed away. I store my scraps in the same place as larger pieces of fabric, and if there is a piece of matching yardage left over, I wrap the scraps inside of it.

As you can imagine, 30 years of quilting has resulted in a rather large fabric collection, so every once in a while it is necessary to evaluate what is in my stash. I have decided to rid myself of any fabrics more than 10 years old by donating them to local quilting groups that make quilts for charities. This practice frees up space for the purchase of new fabrics.

Another way to freshen up your stash and weed out some of the fabrics languishing away is by planning a fabric swap. Each summer one of my quilting groups plans a fabric swap as part of our annual retreat. Everyone brings ten 10" x 10" squares of fabric in a designated color for each person in the group, including herself. After the stacks of fabric are exchanged, you have a wonderful collection of fabrics! The fabrics you bring to swap can be newly purchased or from your own stash. Not only is it a good way to accumulate fabrics for a scrap quilt, but it is also a great solution for a new quilter who feels challenged by a stash that lacks size and variety.

## COLOR PLANS FOR SCRAP QUILTS

Scrap quilts emerged early in the history of quilt-making. Because commercial bedding was not readily available until about 1860, most of the bed coverings were fashioned at home. These were not "best quilts," because they were necessary for warmth; they were referred to as "utility quilts" or scrap quilts. These scrap quilts featured myriad fabrics from leftover clothing, linens, and bedding, and they were not necessarily color coordinated.

My scrap quilts are very carefully planned for color and placement, thus they aren't random scrap quilts in the historical sense of the term. I use a technique that I refer to as a color recipe to plan the fabric placement in my quilts. This technique helps to simplify color selection.

Think in terms of color groups rather than individual colors when using a color recipe. Having chosen a tentative color recipe based on your color preference, select a range of fabrics for each color group in the recipe. If blue is one of the colors, pick several blue prints in differing intensities and visual texture. Pull every blue in your collection that even remotely fits the criteria. Not all of these fabrics will be used, but it is important to study the possibilities. Each color group in the recipe is referred to as a color run.

In planning your recipe, decide which color will be the dark. Which one will be the light? A simple recipe would involve using a constant background fabric in all the blocks and making the design motif in different scrap fabrics. Another recipe would be to change the background fabric in each block as well. This inconsistency adds depth and movement to the simplest quilt design.

Resist overmatching colors and textures. Be sure to use all types of prints. As a color group, reds can range from rust to true red to cranberry and still occupy the same position in the block design. A run of lights can go from a bright white to ecru to beige. If your color runs look boring, throw in a color surprise, such as pink, where only shades of true red have been used. Unique results can occur when you run out of certain fabrics in a color group. This substitution will be interesting rather than jarring and will add variety to your quilt.

Another strategy for making your scrap quilt visually interesting is to vary the contrast in the blocks. High-contrast blocks are needed to establish the design, but more interest will be created when some blocks in the quilt have lower contrast. It's OK to lose the design in some parts of the quilt. You expect the same design to be repeated regularly, and the eye will search for a "disappearing" design motif.

Background fabrics are particularly important in creating variations in the contrast of the blocks. Bright whites can hold the same design spaces in blocks as ecru and more medium tones. The whites will add sparkle to the quilt and lead the eye from one part of the quilt to the next.

## SCRAP-CUTTING STRATEGIES

For each quilt in this book, a materials list specifies the total amount of fabric needed for a particular color group. Pull appropriate amounts of differing fabrics within that color group from your fabric stash. For instance, if three yards of · dark blue fabrics are required, pull half-yard pieces of at least six different blue prints. It sometimes helps to vary the amount of each print used within a color grouping. Some prints are too dominant and eye-catching to be used frequently. Because they interrupt the unity of the quilt, use them in smaller amounts. More restful, smaller-scale prints, which help the design flow from one area of the quilt to another, can be used more frequently.

Next consult the cutting section to see how this fabric is to be cut for the entire quilt. When bias squares are required, they are usually the first cutting specification given, so cut the 8" or 9" squares needed for them first. If the bias squares are constructed of a light fabric and a dark fabric from the same color run, cut the squares from the light prints and then an equal number from the dark prints. When making the bias squares, combine a different light and dark in each set, never repeating the same combination. This will add variety to the quilt.

Use the same procedure when larger squares and triangles are to be cut. If you need 35 dark squares, cut several from each fabric. For instance, if 7 different dark fabrics are used, cut 5 squares from each dark fabric.

As you use these segments in your blocks, be sure to select different color combinations of bias squares as well as triangles and squares of different colors. Vary the emphasis within each block. One block may blend restful prints with low-contrast colors while another offers high contrast with a variety of stripes or polka dots.

When you lay out the blocks for your quilt top, also vary the placement of strong prints and high- and low-contrast blocks. By scattering these elements evenly through your quilt top, you will keep the eye moving, encouraging the viewer to look at the quilt longer. Or you may want to group all the low-contrast blocks or soft colors in one area of the quilt, creating a flow into stronger contrast or brighter color. Each step of the quilt construction will give you the opportunity to make new design choices and add more individuality.

Study the alternative color scheme that follows each quilt to help you think of new design ideas. This quilt or project always varies in color but may also vary in size, setting plan, or border options. Have fun adding your own creative ideas to make a quilt that is uniquely yours.

## KEEP ON GOING

When making scrap quilts, don't think scrappy only in terms of your blocks. I also like to use a scrap approach when choosing sashing for a quilt. If you're making scrappy sashing, use at least five different fabrics. This will add variety in the quilt and minimize the same fabric being repeated too close to itself.

And what better place to use scraps of fabric than on the quilt backing? The backing of "Corner Star" (page 96) was made with fabrics left over from the quilt top.

Backing of "Corner Star"

# Tools of the Trade

Quiltmaking, whether you're using scraps or not, requires some basic tools. The following is a list of items I use each time I make a project.

**Rotary cutter and mat:** A large rotary cutter enables you to quickly cut strips and pieces without templates. A cutting mat is essential to protect both the blade and the table on which you're cutting. An 18" x 24" mat allows you to cut long strips, on the straight or bias grain. You might also consider purchasing a smaller mat to use when working with scraps.

Use a clear acrylic ruler to measure fabric and guide the rotary cutter. It is possible to cut quilt pieces with any see-through ruler that you have, and you can also adapt a general-purpose ruler to cut bias squares. It is easier, however, to use the special rulers that I recommend. They contain only the cutting lines and strategic alignment guides necessary to keep the fabric grain

line in the correct position. Because you don't have to visually screen out unnecessary lines, your eyes can quickly focus on only the lines you need. Using a specialized ruler improves cutting accuracy, makes quiltmaking more fun, and frees you from the matching and stitching frustrations that can result from inaccurate cuts.

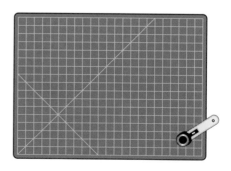

**Rotary-cutting rulers:** Use a see-through ruler to measure and guide the rotary cutter. There are many appropriate rulers on the market. Make sure the one you choose includes markings for 45° and 60° angles, and guidelines for cutting strips in standard-size measurements. Select a ruler that is marked with large, clear numbers and does not have a lot of confusing lines.

The Bias Square® ruler is critical for cutting accurate bias squares. This acrylic ruler is available in three sizes: 4", 6", or 8" square, and is ruled with ⅛" markings. It features a diagonal line, which is placed on the bias seam, enabling you to cut an accurately sewn square that looks as if it were made from two triangles.

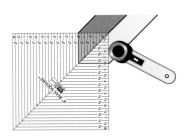

The Bias Square is also convenient to use when cutting small quilt pieces, such as squares, rectangles, and triangles. The larger 8" size is ideal for quickly cutting blocks that require large squares and triangles as well as for making diagonal cuts for half-square and quarter-square triangles. A 20-cm-square metric version is also available. If you cannot locate these rulers at your local quilt or fabric shop, they can be ordered from Martingale & Company (www.martingale-pub.com).

**Sewing machine:** Stitching quilts on a sewing machine is easy and enjoyable. Spend some time getting to know your machine and become comfortable with its use. Keep your machine dust-free and well oiled.

Machine piecing does not require an elaborate sewing machine. All you need is a straight-stitch machine in good working order. It should make an evenly locked straight stitch that looks the same on both sides of the seam. Adjust the tension, if necessary, to produce smooth, even seams. A puckered seam causes the fabric to curve, distorting the size and shape of the piecing and the quilt you're making.

**Pins:** A good supply of glass- or plastic-headed pins is necessary. Long pins are especially helpful when pinning thick layers together. If you plan to machine quilt, you will need to hold the layers of the quilt together with a large supply of rustproof, size 2 safety pins.

**Iron and ironing board:** Frequent and careful pressing is necessary to ensure a smooth, accurately stitched quilt top. Place your iron and ironing board, along with a plastic spray bottle of water, close to your sewing machine.

**Needles:** Use sewing-machine needles sized for cotton fabrics (size 70/10 or 80/12). You also need hand-sewing needles (Sharps) and hand-quilting needles (Betweens #8, #9, and #10).

**Scissors:** Use good-quality shears, and use them only for cutting fabric. Thread snips or embroidery scissors are handy for clipping stray threads.

**Seam ripper:** This little tool will come in handy if you find it necessary to remove a seam before resewing.

# Fabric Essentials

Fabric is the most important "tool" in the quilt-making process, but it is also a very subjective part of your quilt. Each individual gravitates toward particular colors and different ways of preparing the fabric. In this section, I share general information about selecting fabrics, yardage requirements, and how to prepare your fabrics before you begin sewing.

## FABRIC SELECTION

Your fabric and color choices will depend on what appeals to you, what is available in your scrap bag, or what fat quarters or fat eighths you have purchased.

If you have trouble deciding on a color scheme, select a color-coordinated bundle of fat quarters or fat eighths. Often this can be the basis for an effective color scheme. Supplement with scraps from your stash and the purchase of additional background fabric, and you're on your way. You can also purchase more of a particular fabric that you wish to predominate in your quilt. For instance, if the fabric requirements call for six fat quarters of dark fabric, purchase three fat quarters of a dark print that you really like and one fat quarter each of three other dark fabrics.

To maintain a scrappy effect, most of the quilts shown in this book don't use a single light print as a background but a combination of fabrics that are similar in color and value. Study the differences in these quilts

and see which you prefer. If you prefer the look of a single light background fabric, simply convert the yardage given in fat quarters to yards. To do this, divide the number of fat quarters by four. For example, 14 fat quarters equals 3½ yards of fabric.

For best results, be sure your scraps and any required yardage that you purchase are closely

woven, 100%-cotton fabrics. Fabrics with a polyester content may make small patchwork pieces difficult to cut and sew accurately.

If your quilt pattern has a common background fabric on which the design is set, select the background fabric first. Choose a background print that is nondirectional and still appears unified after being cut apart and resewn. Don't limit your choices to solid colors, even though muslin is a traditional background fabric for scrap quilts. If you really want to use a solid-colored fabric, try a deep turkey red or perhaps black or navy blue for an Amish look. Remember, solid-colored fabrics tend to emphasize mismatched seams and irregular quilting stitches. If you're a beginner and are still perfecting your piecing and quilting skills, select a print that is more likely to hide minor imperfections.

To test the suitability of background fabrics while shopping, make several directional folds and evaluate the unity of the design.

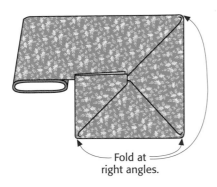

Fold at right angles.

Prints with a white background have a clean, formal look; those with a beige or tan background resemble antique quilts and have a more informal look.

Once you have chosen the background fabric, select the remaining fabrics that will enhance the background fabric. Study the colors in the background-fabric design and begin your selection. Because you will be working with scraps, you will use a number of different fabrics to represent a single value. When cutting the pieces shown as dark in the quilt plan, for example, you can use two, three, or a dozen different dark fabrics.

These might all be the same color (such as an assortment of reds) or different colors of the same value (such as a combination of dark blues, dark greens, and browns).

If you're using fabric randomly, don't worry about the placement of stripes or plaids. Let them fall as they are cut, including off-grain plaids. Stripes can be used both horizontally and vertically in the same block.

Controlling the direction of striped fabric or directional prints requires careful cutting and placement. For example, in cutting half-square triangles, cut half the triangles in one direction and the remaining triangles in the opposite direction.

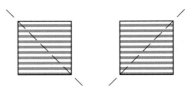

When sewing these pieces to a square or diamond, stitch the triangles from squares cut in one direction to opposite sides of the center square.

Then sew the pieces from squares cut in the opposite direction to the remaining sides of the center square.

To center a design from a pictorial or theme print, use a see-through ruler and adjust the crosswise cuts to center the design.

Many novelty prints require special cutting to show them to their best advantage. I take the time to fussy cut these fabrics for my quilts, knowing that the results are well worth the effort, even though the remaining fabric looks like a piece of Swiss cheese when I am finished.

The individual motifs and vignettes printed on these fabrics are ideal candidates for fussy cutting.

To fussy cut a fabric, make an expandable window from two pieces of L-shaped cardboard. Place this window on the different design elements in the fabric, noting the size needed to accommodate each design. Look for a common size that will work for most of the designs; unfortunately, not all the motifs may be the same size. Once you determine a common size, add ¼"-wide seam allowances on all sides and cut the necessary pieces.

# YARDAGE REQUIREMENTS

While the scrappy projects in this book are made of multiple fabrics, yardage is required for some pieces, such as background pieces, borders, and backings. The fabric requirements are generous and based on yardage that is 42" wide after prewashing. If your fabric is wider than 42", there will be a little left over at the end of your strips. If your fabric is narrower than 42", you may need to cut an extra strip. Save any extra yardage or strips for future scrap quilts.

The yardage amounts for other pieces will specify fat quarters rather than "scraps." A fat quarter is an 18" x 22" piece of fabric as opposed to the standard quarter yard that is cut selvage to selvage and measures 9" x 42". The fat quarter provides a more convenient size to use, especially when cutting bias strips for bias squares. Another common size is the fat eighth, which measures 9" x 22".

If your "scraps" aren't as large as a fat quarter or fat eighth, or you wish to use more fabrics than indicated in the instructions, look at the cutting instructions to see what pieces are cut from that color group and then cut the appropriate amount from your scraps.

# FABRIC PREPARATION

If you normally wash your fabrics before using them, scraps left over from previous projects will probably need nothing more than a little ironing to eliminate a few wrinkles. Any new fabric purchases or unwashed fabrics gleaned from your stash should be washed first to preshrink, test for colorfastness, and get rid of excess dye. Continue to wash fabric until the rinse water is completely clear. Add a square of white fabric to each washing of the fabric. When this white fabric remains its original color, the fabric is colorfast. A cupful of vinegar in the rinse water can also be used to help set difficult dyes.

In this section, you'll find instructions for the construction techniques used throughout the book.

## SCRAPPY STRIP SETS AND NINE-PATCH UNITS

Strip piecing eliminates the long and tedious repetition of sewing small individual pieces together; however, it usually produces many identical units. In a scrap quilt, it is preferable that your strip-pieced units contain a variety of fabrics. I use the following techniques when making strip sets so that I can achieve the scrappy look without cutting individual pieces.

- Cut half strips of fabric (20" to 22" wide) rather than full-length strips (40" to 44" wide).

- Cut all the light strips from a variety of light fabrics rather than a single fabric.

- Cut all the dark strips from a variety of dark fabrics rather than a single fabric.

- Select a different combination of strip-set segments for each block that you make.

## Strip Sets

Each project will indicate the number of strips to cut from the appropriate fabrics. Cut these strips on the crosswise grain.

1. Refer to the project instructions to sew the strips together along the long edges. Press the seams toward the darker fabric, pressing from the right side so the fabric won't pleat along the seam lines.

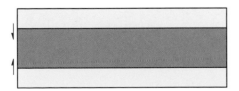

2. Straighten the right end of each strip set by aligning a horizontal line of the cutting ruler with one of the strip set's internal seams. Cut along the right edge of the ruler. Place the straightened end on the left, align the desired measurement on your cutting ruler with the straightened end, and cut.

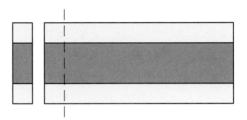

## Nine-Patch Units

1. Make the strip sets as indicated in the project instructions, varying the prints used in the light and dark positions. You will have one strip set that is made from one light strip and two dark strips (strip set 1), and one strip set that is made from one dark strip and two light strips (strip set 2). Make as many different strip set combinations as possible with the required fabrics.

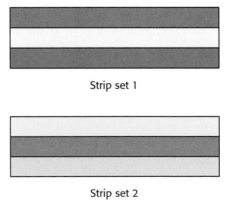

Strip set 1

Strip set 2

2. Cut the strip sets into segments the width indicated in the project instructions.

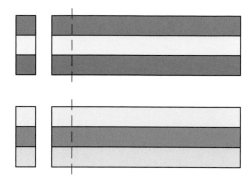

3. Stitch two different strip set 2 segments to each side of a strip set 1 segment as shown. Press the seams toward the strip set 2 segments.

# BASIC BIAS SQUARE TECHNIQUE

Many traditional quilt patterns contain squares made from two contrasting half-square triangles. The short sides of the triangles are on the straight grain of fabric while the long sides are on the bias. These are called bias-square units. Using a bias strip-piecing method, you can easily sew and cut large amounts of bias squares. This technique is especially useful for small bias squares, for which pressing after stitching usually distorts the shape (and sometimes results in burned fingers).

**Note:** All instructions in this book give the cut size for bias squares; the finished size after stitching will be ½" smaller.

To make bias squares:

1. Start with two squares of fabric. The instructions in this book call for a pair of 8" x 8" or 9" x 9" squares. Layer the squares right sides up and cut in half diagonally.

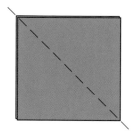

2. Cut the squares into strips the width indicated in the instructions, measuring from the previous cut.

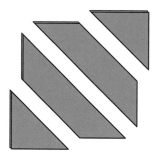

3. Stitch the strips together using ¼"-wide seams. Be sure to align the strips so the lower edge and one adjacent edge form straight lines.

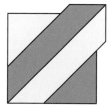
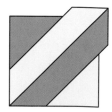

4. Starting at the lower-left corner, align the 45° mark of the Bias Square ruler on the seam line. Each bias square will require two cuts.

The first cut is along the side and the top edge. It removes the bias square from the rest of the fabric and is made slightly larger than the correct size, as shown in the series of illustrations below.

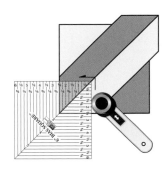

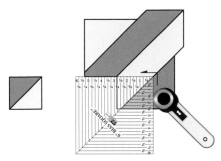

Align 45° mark on seam line
and cut first 2 sides.

5. The second cut is made along the remaining two sides. It aligns the diagonal and trims the bias square to the correct size. To make the cut, turn the segment and place the Bias Square on the opposite two sides, aligning the required measurements on both sides of the cutting guide and the 45° mark on the seam. Cut the remaining two sides of the bias squares.

Turn cut segments and
cut opposite 2 sides.

6. Continue cutting bias squares from each unit in this manner, working from left to right and from bottom to top, row by row, until you have cut bias squares from all usable fabric. Use the chart below to determine strip width and how many bias squares you can expect to cut from two squares of fabric.

| Finished Size | Cut Size | Fabric Size | Strip Width | Yield |
|---|---|---|---|---|
| 2" | 2½" x 2½" | 8" x 8"* | 2½" | 8 |
| 2" | 2½" x 2½" | 9" x 9" | 2½" | 14 |
| 2⅛" | 2⅝" x 2⅝" | 8" x 8" | 2½" | 8 |
| 2½" | 3" x 3" | 8" x 8" | 2¾" | 8 |
| 2½" | 3" x 3" | 9" x 9" | 2¾" | 8 |
| 3" | 3½" x 3½" | 9" x 9" | 3" | 8 |

*A pair of 7" x 7" squares will yield the same number of bias squares.

# Machine Piecing

It's important to be comfortable with the sewing machine you're using. If this is your first machine-made quilt, practice guiding fabric through the machine. If you leave the machine unthreaded, you can practice over and over on the same pieces of fabric.

Operating a sewing machine requires the same type of coordination it takes to drive a car. Use your foot to control the machine's speed and your hands to control the fabric's direction. To start, use your right foot for the foot pedal to manage the speed. If the machine goes too fast at first, slip a sponge under a hinge-type pedal to slow it down. Use your hands to guide the fabric that feeds into the machine.

A good habit to develop is to use a seam ripper or long pin to gently guide the fabric up to the needle. You can hold seam intersections together or make minor adjustments before the fabric is sewn.

The most important skill in machine piecing is sewing an accurate ¼"-wide seam. This is necessary for seams to match and for the resulting block or quilt to measure the required size. There are several methods that will help you achieve this.

- Purchase a special foot that is sized so that you can align the edge of your fabric with the edge of the presser foot, resulting in a seam that is ¼" from the fabric edge. Bernina has a special patchwork foot (#37) and Little Foot makes several special ¼" feet that fit most machines.

- If you have an electronic or computerized sewing machine, adjust the needle position so that the resulting seam is ¼" from the fabric edge.

- Find the ¼" seam allowance on your machine by placing an accurate template under the presser foot and lowering the needle onto the seam line; mark the seam allowance by placing a piece of masking tape at the edge of the

template. You can use several layers of masking tape, building up a raised edge to guide your fabric. You can also use a piece of moleskin for a raised seam guide.

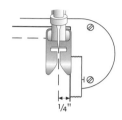

Test to make sure that the method you're using results in an accurate ¼"-wide seam.

1. Cut three strips of fabric, 1½" x 3".

2. Sew the strips together, using the edge of the presser foot or the seam guide you have made.

3. Press seams toward the outer edges. After sewing and pressing, the center strip should measure exactly 1" wide. If it doesn't, adjust the needle or seam guide in the proper direction.

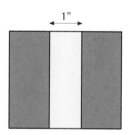

## Matching Seams

When sewing the fabric pieces that make up a unit or block, follow the piecing diagram provided. Press each group of pieces before joining it to the next unit.

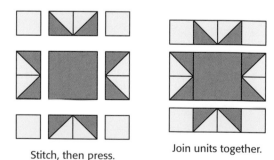

Stitch, then press.          Join units together.

There are several techniques you can use to get your seams to match perfectly.

**Opposing seams:** When stitching one seamed unit to another, press seams that need to match in opposite directions. The two "opposing" seams will hold each other in place and evenly distribute the fabric bulk. Plan pressing to take advantage of opposing seams.

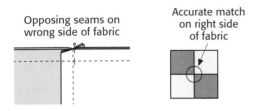

Opposing seams on wrong side of fabric

Accurate match on right side of fabric

**Positioning pin:** A pin, carefully pushed straight through two points that need to match, will establish the proper matching point. Pin the remainder of the seam normally and remove the positioning pin just before stitching.

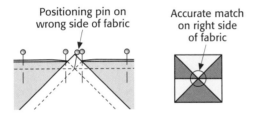

Positioning pin on wrong side of fabric

Accurate match on right side of fabric

**The X:** When triangles are pieced, the stitches will form an X at the next seam line. Stitch through the center of the X to make sure the points on the sewn triangles will not be cut off.

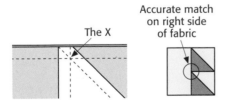

The X

Accurate match on right side of fabric

**Easing:** When two pieces you're sewing together are supposed to match but are slightly different in length, pin the points to match and stitch with the shorter piece on top. The feed dogs will ease the fullness of the bottom piece.

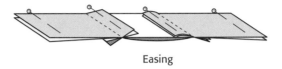

Easing

Inspect each intersection from the right side to see that it is matched. If the seams don't meet accurately, note which direction the fabric needs to be moved. Use a seam ripper to rip out the seam intersection and ½" of stitching on either side of the intersection. Shift fabric to correct the alignment, place positioning pins, and then restitch.

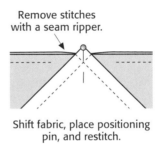

Remove stitches with a seam ripper.

Shift fabric, place positioning pin, and restitch.

**Pressing:** After stitching a seam, it is important to press your work. Careful pressing helps make the next steps in the stitching process, such as matching points or aligning seams, easier.

Be sure to press, not iron, your work. Ironing is an aggressive back-and-forth motion that we use on clothing to remove wrinkles. This action can easily pull and distort the bias edges or seams in your piecing. Perfectly marked and sewn quilt pieces are commonly distorted by excessive ironing. You may notice this particularly after ironing a square made from what had been two perfectly marked, cut, and sewn triangles. Many times the finished unit is no longer square after you've ironed it. Pressing is the gentle lowering, pressing, and lifting of the iron along the length of the fabric without moving the iron back and forth along the seam. Let the heat, steam, and an occasional spritz of water press the fabric in the desired direction.

## Matching Blocks

After you make the required number of blocks, assemble them into rows. The blocks in each row should be pinned together at strategic intersections to ensure accurate matching as rows are sewn together. The process is similar to matching seams within a block.

To make this process easier, plan for opposing seams when you press blocks after stitching. Press seams in opposite directions from row to row.

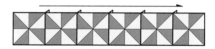

Row 1 – Press seams to right.

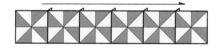

Row 2 – Press seams to left.

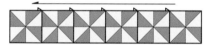

Row 3 – Press seams to right.

If the blocks have points, such as the Pinwheel blocks shown, the points of adjoining blocks should meet ¼" from the raw edge.

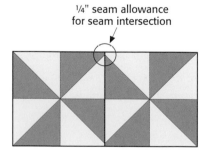

¼" seam allowance for seam intersection

Use positioning pins to hold seam allowances in place. Remove the pins before stitching through the seam intersection.

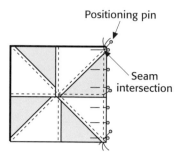

Positioning pin

Seam intersection

## Chain Piecing

Chain piecing is an assembly-line approach to putting your blocks together. Rather than sewing each block from start to finish, you can sew identical units of each block together at one time, streamlining the process. It's a good idea, however, to sew one sample block together from start to finish to ensure that the pieces have been accurately cut and that you have the proper positioning and coloration for each piece.

Stack the units you will be sewing in pairs, arranging any opposing seam allowances so that the top seam allowance faces toward the needle and the lower seam allowance faces toward you. Then you won't need to keep checking to see if the lower seam is being pulled to the wrong side by the feed dogs as you feed the fabric through the sewing machine.

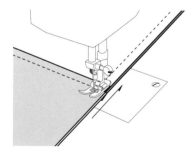

Face top seam allowance toward the needle whenever possible.

Feed units through the machine without stopping to cut thread. There will be a "stitch" or small length of thread between the units.

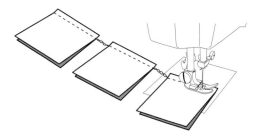

Take the connected units to the ironing board for pressing, and then clip them apart. Chain piecing takes a little planning, but it saves you time and thread.

Keep a stack of fabric scraps, about 2" x 2", near your machine. When you begin to sew, fold one of the squares in half and sew to its edge. This folded piece of fabric is called a *thread saver*. Leave the presser foot down and continue sewing onto your piecing unit. When you have finished sewing a seam or chain piecing, sew onto another thread saver, leaving the needle in place and the presser foot down. Cut the chain-pieced units away from the thread saver under the presser foot. This thread saver will be in place for sewing the next seam or unit.

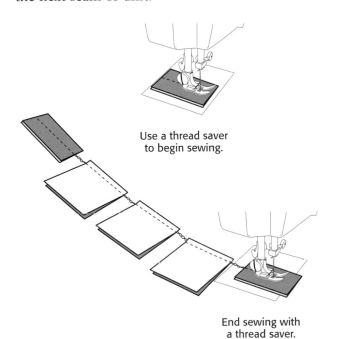

Use a thread saver
to begin sewing.

End sewing with
a thread saver.

This technique saves thread because you don't stop and pull a length of thread to remove fabric from the machine. All the tails of thread will be on the thread saver and not on the back of the block or quilt. This method also keeps the machine from eating the edges of the fabric as you start a seam.

# APPLIQUÉ

Some of the quilts in this book have appliquéd accents. Use the paper-patch technique for all of the pieces except stems. For stems, use the bias-stem method.

## Paper-Patch Appliqué

1. Using a sturdy material, such as cardboard or template plastic, make a template of each shape in the appliqué design. Don't add seam allowances to the templates.

2. On bond-weight paper or freezer paper, trace around the stiffened templates to make a paper patch for each shape in the appliqué.

3. Pin or iron each paper patch to the wrong side of the fabric. If using freezer paper, pin with the plastic-coated side facing up.

4. Cut out the fabric shapes, adding a ⅛"-wide seam allowance around each paper shape.

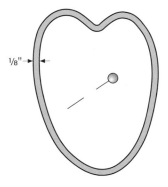

⅛"

5. With your fingers, turn the seam allowance over the edge of the paper and baste to the paper. Clip corners and do inside curves first. (A little clipping may be necessary to help the fabric stretch.) On outside curves, take small running stitches through the fabric only, to ease in fullness.

For points, such as the tips of the leaves in "Pot of Flowers," first fold the point to the inside. Then fold the remaining seam allowances over the paper.

Fold corners to inside.

Fold remaining seam allowances over paper.

6. When all the seam allowances are turned and basted, press the appliqué pieces. Then position and pin the pieces in place on the background fabric.

7. Use a small blind hem stitch and a single strand of thread that matches the appliqué (for example, pink thread for a pink heart) to appliqué shapes to the background fabric.

8. Start the first stitch from the back of the block. Bring the needle up through the background fabric and through the folded edge of the appliqué piece.

9. Insert the needle right next to where you brought it up, but this time put it through only the background fabric.

10. Bring the needle up through the background fabric and then into the appliqué piece, approximately ⅛" or less from the first stitch.

11. Space your stitches a little less than ⅛" apart.

12. When appliqué is complete, slit the background fabric behind the appliqué shape and pull out the paper patch.

## Bias Stems

Bias stems are easy to make with the help of metal or nylon bias press bars, also called Celtic bars. These handy notions are available at most quilt shops. The following steps describe the process of making bias stems.

1. Cut the fabric indicated in the materials list for the stems into bias strips the width indicated in the instructions.

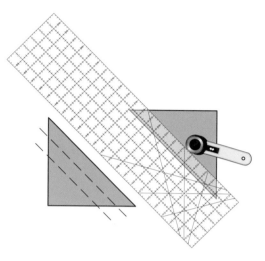

2. Fold each bias strip in half, wrong sides together, and stitch ⅛" from the long raw edges to form a tube.

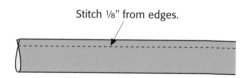

Stitch ⅛" from edges.

3. Insert the appropriate size of bias bar into the tube, roll the seam to the underside, and press flat. Remove the bias bar.

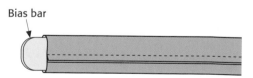

Bias bar

4. Cut the bias tube to the lengths needed and place them on the background fabric, forming the desired shape. Pin (or baste) and appliqué the pieces in place.

# Finishing Techniques

This section includes tips for completing a quilt with confidence and pride. What I suggest works well for me but is by no means the only way to accomplish the job. If a technique is new to you, try it; you might find that you incorporate the technique into your quiltmaking process from now on.

## ADDING BORDERS

Borders can be used to frame and soften a busy design. They are also helpful in enlarging a quilt to fit a standard-sized bed. It isn't always necessary to have a border on a quilt, however. Many antique quilts made from scraps have no borders, since continuous yardage was scarce and expensive.

Straighten the edges of your quilt top before adding borders. There should be little or no trimming needed for a straight-set quilt.

To find the correct measurement for straight-cut border strips, always measure through the center of the quilt, not at the outside edges. This ensures that the borders are of equal length on opposite sides of the quilt and brings the outer edges in line with the center dimension if discrepancies exist. Otherwise, your quilt might not be "square" due to minor piecing variations and/or stretching that occurred while you worked with the pieces. If there is a large size difference between the two sides, it is better to go back and correct the source of the problem rather than try to make the border fit and end up with a distorted quilt.

### Borders with Straight-Cut Corners

The easiest border to add is a straight-cut border. This method has been used on almost all the quilts with borders in this book. You will save

fabric if you attach the border strips to the longest sides first, and then stitch the border strips to the remaining two sides.

1. Measure the length of the quilt through the center. Cut two border strips to this measurement.

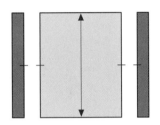

Measure center of quilt,
top to bottom.
Mark centers.

For the quilts in this book, border strips cut on the crosswise grain will need to be pieced together first and then cut to the exact size. Border strips cut on the lengthwise grain are cut longer than necessary to allow for any variances in the quilt-top size. Cut them to the exact size before adding to the quilt top.

## ANGLED SEAMS

When joining border strips, the seam will be less noticeable and stronger if it is pieced on an angle.

Trim.

Press seam open.

2. Mark the centers of the border strips and the quilt top. Pin the borders to the sides of the quilt, matching centers and ends and easing or slightly stretching the quilt to fit the border strip as necessary.

3. Sew the side borders in place and press the seams toward the borders.

4. Measure the width of the quilt through the center, including the side borders, to determine the length of the top and bottom borders. Cut the border strips to this measurement, piecing strips as necessary. Mark the centers of the border strips and the quilt top. Pin borders to the top and bottom of the quilt top, easing or slightly stretching the quilt to fit as necessary.

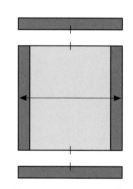

Measure center of quilt,
side to side, including borders.
Mark centers.

5. Sew the top and bottom borders in place and press the seams toward the borders.

## Borders with Mitered Corners

Mitered borders have a diagonal seam where the borders meet in the corners. If your quilt has multiple borders, sew the individual strips together and treat the resulting unit as a single border.

1. First estimate the finished outside dimensions of your quilt, including borders. Cut border strips to this length plus at least ½" for seam allowances. Add 2" to 3" to be safer and to give some leeway.

2. Mark the center of the quilt edges and the border strips.

3. Measure the length and width of the quilt top through the center.

4. Place a pin at each end of the side borders to mark the length of the quilt top. Repeat with the top and bottom borders.

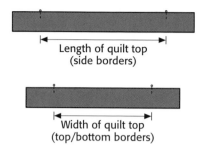

Length of quilt top
(side borders)

Width of quilt top
(top/bottom borders)

5. Pin the side borders to the quilt top, matching the centers. Line up the pins at either end of the border strips with the quilt edges. Stitch, beginning and ending the stitching ¼" from the raw edges of the quilt top. Repeat with the remaining borders.

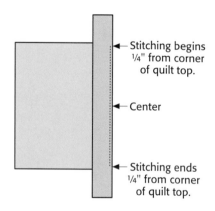

Stitching begins
¼" from corner
of quilt top.

Center

Stitching ends
¼" from corner
of quilt top.

6. Lay the first corner to be mitered on the ironing board. Fold under one border at a 45° angle to the other. Press and pin.

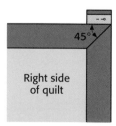

45°

Right side
of quilt

7. Fold the quilt with right sides together, lining up the edges of the border. If necessary, use a ruler and pencil to draw a line on the crease

to make the line more visible. Stitch on the pressed crease, sewing from the corner to the outside edges.

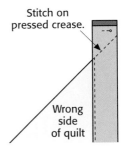

Stitch on pressed crease.

Wrong side of quilt

8. Press the seam open and trim the excess from the borders, leaving a ¼"-wide seam allowance.

9. Repeat with the remaining corners.

## MARKING THE QUILTING DESIGN

Whether you machine or hand quilt, you'll need to mark a quilting design on the quilt top. The exceptions are when you're stitching in the ditch, outlining the design ¼" away from all seams, stitching a grid of straight lines using masking tape as a guide, or stitching a meandering, free-motion design.

- To stitch in the ditch, place the stitches in the valley created next to the seam. Stitch on the side that does not have the seam allowance under it.

Quilting in the ditch

- To outline a design, stitch ¼" from the seam inside each shape.

Outline quilting

- To mark a grid or pattern of lines, use ¼"-wide masking tape in 15" to 18" lengths. Place strips of tape on a small area and quilt next to the edge of the tape. Remove the tape when stitching is complete. You can reuse the tape to mark another area. *Caution:* Don't leave tape on a quilt top for an extended length of time, as it may leave a sticky residue.

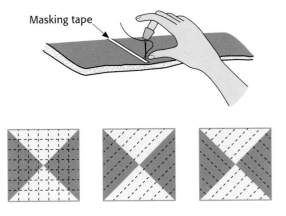

Masking tape

- To mark complex designs, use a stencil. Quilting stencils made from durable plastic are available in quilt shops. Use stencils to mark repeated designs. There is a groove cut into the plastic, wide enough to allow the use of a marking device. Just place the marker inside the groove to quickly transfer the design to the fabric. Good removable marking pencils include Berol silver pencils, EZ Washout marking pencils, mechanical pencils, and sharp regular pencils. Just be sure to draw lines lightly. Always test any marking device on a scrap of fabric for removability.

## BACKING

For most quilts larger than crib size, you will need to piece the backing from two or more strips of fabric if you use 42"-wide fabric. Seams can run horizontally or vertically in a pieced backing, as long as the fabric isn't a directional print. Avoid the temptation to use a bed sheet for a backing, as it is difficult to quilt through. Cut backing 3" to 4" larger than the quilt top all around. Be sure to trim away the selvages where pieces are joined.

Plan to put a sleeve or rod pocket on the back of the quilt so you can hang it. (See "Quilt Sleeves" on page 31.) Purchase extra backing fabric so that the sleeve and the backing match. Once you know the finished size of your quilt, refer to the following illustrations to plan the backing layout and to determine how much fabric you'll need.

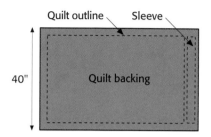

One fabric length:
For quilts up to 40" width or length
Example: 60" (length or width) +
18" (½ yard for trimming and sleeve) =
78" (2⅛ yards)

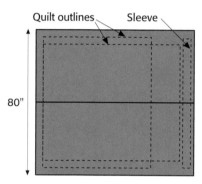

Two fabric lengths:
For quilts up to 80" width or length
Example: 2 x 100" (length or width) =
200" + 27" (¾ yard for trimming and sleeve) =
227" (6⅓ yards)

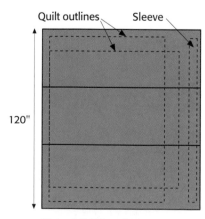

Three fabric lengths:
For quilts up to 120" width or length
Example: 3 x 100" = 300" + 36"
(1 yard for trimming and sleeve) =
336" (9⅓ yards)

Sometimes the backing fabric is a little too narrow for a 45"-wide quilt. Pieced backs are fun to make, and they can be the answer to this annoying problem.

You can also use scraps of fabric from your stash, piecing them together to form a backing large enough for your quilt top. This is most effective when you use some of the fabrics that were used on the front of the quilt.

# BATTING

There are many types of batting to choose from. Select a high-loft batting for a bed quilt that you want to look puffy. Lightweight battings are fine for baby quilts or wall hangings. A lightweight batting is easier to quilt through and shows the quilting design well. It also gives your quilt an antique, old-fashioned look.

Polyester batting works well, doesn't shift after washing, and is easy to quilt through. It comes in lightweight and regular lofts as well as in fat, or high-loft, batting for comforters.

Cotton batting is a good choice if you're quilting an old quilt top or if you want to achieve the look of a vintage quilt. This batting must be quilted with stitches no more than 2" apart.

Dark batting works well behind a dark quilt top. If there is any bearding (batting fibers creeping through the top), it will not be as noticeable.

# LAYERING AND BASTING

Open a package of batting and smooth it out flat. Allow the batting to rest in this position for at least 24 hours. Press the backing so that all seams are flat and the fold lines have been removed.

A large dining-room table, Ping-Pong table, or two large folding tables pushed together make an ideal work surface on which to prepare your quilt. Use a table pad to protect your dining-room table. The floor is not a good choice for layering your quilt. It requires you to do too much bending, and the layers can easily shift or be disturbed.

Place the backing on the table with the wrong side of the fabric facing up. If the table is large enough, you may want to tape the backing down with masking tape. Spread your batting over the backing, centering it, and smooth out any remaining folds.

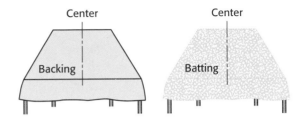

Center the freshly pressed and marked quilt top on these two layers. Check all four sides to make sure there is adequate batting and backing. Stretch the backing to make sure it is still smooth.

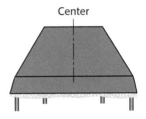

The basting method you use depends on whether you will quilt by hand or machine. Thread basting is used for hand quilting, while safety-pin basting is generally used for machine quilting.

## Thread Basting

Starting in the center of the quilt top, baste the three layers together with straight pins while gently smoothing out the fullness to the sides and corners. Take care not to distort the borders and any straight lines within the quilt design.

After pinning, baste the layers together with a needle and light-colored thread, so the thread color won't bleed onto the quilt. Start in the middle and make a line of long stitches to each corner to form a large X.

Continue basting in a grid of parallel lines 6" to 8" apart. Finish with a row of basting around the outside edges. Quilts that are to be quilted with a hoop or on your lap will be handled more

than those quilted on a frame; therefore, they require more basting. After basting, remove the pins. Now you're ready to quilt.

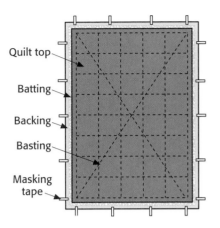

## Pin Basting

A quick way to baste a quilt top for machine quilting is with size 2 safety pins. They are large enough to catch all three layers but not so large that they snag fine fabric. Begin pinning in the center and work out toward the edges. Place pins 4" to 5" apart.

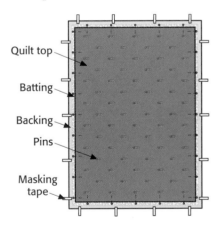

Use long, straight pins along the outside edge to hold everything in place. Place pins perpendicular to the edge, 1½" to 2" apart. Remove the straight pins before quilting.

# Hand Quilting

To quilt by hand, you need quilting thread, quilting needles, small scissors, a thimble, and perhaps a balloon or large rubber band to help grasp the needle if it gets stuck. Quilt on a frame, a large hoop, or on your lap or a table. Use a single strand of quilting thread not longer than 18". Make a small, single knot at the end of the thread. The quilting stitch is a small running stitch that goes through all three layers of the quilt. Take two, three, or even four stitches at a time if you can keep them even. When crossing seams, you might find it necessary to "hunt and peck" one stitch at a time.

To begin, insert the needle in the top layer about 1" from the point where you want to start stitching. Pull the needle out at the desired starting point and gently tug at the knot until it pops through the fabric and is buried in the batting. Make a backstitch and begin quilting. Stitches should be tiny (8 to 10 per inch is good), even, and straight; tiny stitches will come with practice.

When you come almost to the end of the thread, make a single knot ¼" from the fabric. Take a backstitch to bury the knot in the batting. Run the thread off through the batting and out the quilt top; then snip it off. The first and last stitches will look different from the running stitches in between. To make them less noticeable, start and stop where quilting lines cross each other or at seam joints. Remove the basting when the quilting is finished.

Hand-quilting stitch

# Machine Quilting

Machine quilting is a good choice for those who have little time and need to finish their tops in a hurry. It's also a practical choice for baby quilts or other items that will need lots of washing.

Machine quilting works best on small projects; it can be frustrating to feed the bulk of a large quilt through a sewing machine.

Use a walking foot or even-feed foot (or the built-in, even-feed feature, when available) for your sewing machine to help the quilt layers feed through the machine without shifting or puckering. This type of foot is essential for straight-line and grid quilting and for large, simple curves. Read your machine's instruction manual for special tension settings to sew through extra fabric thicknesses.

Walking foot

Curved designs require free fabric movement under the foot of the sewing machine. This is called free-motion quilting, and with a little practice, you can imitate beautiful hand quilting designs quickly. If you wish to quilt curved designs with your machine, use a darning foot and lower the feed dogs while using this foot. Because the feed dogs are lowered for free-motion quilting, the speed at which you run the machine and feed the fabric under the foot determines the stitch length. Practice running the machine fairly fast, since this makes it easier to sew smoother lines of quilting. With free-motion quilting, don't turn the fabric under the needle. Instead, guide the fabric as if the needle were a stationary pencil drawing the lines of your design.

Darning foot

Practice first on a piece of fabric until you get the feel of controlling the motion of the fabric with your hands. Stitch some free-form scribbles, zigzags, and curves. Try a heart or a star. Then practice on a sample block with batting and backing. Make sure your chair is adjusted to a comfortable height. This type of quilting may feel awkward at first, but with a little determination and practice you will be able to complete a project with beautiful machine quilting in just a few hours.

Keep the spacing between quilting lines consistent over the entire quilt. Avoid using complex, little designs and leaving large unquilted spaces. For most battings, a 2" or 3" square is the largest area that can be left unquilted. Read the instructions enclosed with the batting you have chosen.

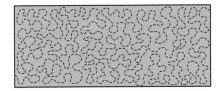

Don't try to machine quilt an entire quilt in one sitting, even if it's a small project. Break the work into short periods, and stretch and relax your muscles regularly.

When all the quilting has been completed, remove the safety pins. Sometimes it is necessary to remove safety pins as you work.

## BINDING THE EDGES

My favorite quilt binding is a double-layer French binding made from bias strips. It rolls over the edges of the quilt nicely, and the two layers of fabric resist wear. If you use 2¼"-wide strips, the finished width of this binding will be ⅜".

Double-layer French binding

The quilt instructions tell you how much fabric to purchase for binding. If, however, you enlarge your quilt or need to compute binding fabric, use the following handy chart.

| Length of Binding | Fabric Needed |
|---|---|
| 115" | ¼ yard* |
| 180" | ⅜ yard |
| 255" | ½ yard |
| 320" | ⅝ yard |
| 400" | ¾ yard |
| 465" | ⅞ yard |

*It's a good idea to purchase ½ yard of fabric instead of ¼ yard so the bias strips will be longer and the binding won't have as many seams.

Determine the distance around your quilt and add about 10" for turning the corners and for overlapping the ends of the binding strips.

After quilting, trim excess batting and backing even with the edge of the quilt top. A rotary cutter and long ruler will ensure accurate straight edges. If the basting is no longer in place, baste all three layers together at the outer edges. If you intend to attach a sleeve or rod pocket, make one now to attach with the binding. See "Quilt Sleeves" on page 31 for instructions.

To cut bias strips for binding, follow these steps:

1. Align the 45° marking of a Bias Square along the selvage and place a long ruler's edge against it. Make the first cut.

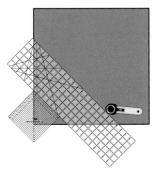

2. Measure the desired width of the strip (2¼") from the cut edge of the fabric. Cut along the edge with the ruler. Continue cutting until you have the number of strips necessary to achieve the required binding length.

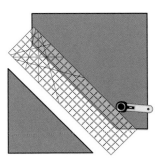

Sometimes a 24"-long ruler may be too short for some of the cuts. The fabric can be folded to accommodate the ruler. After making several cuts, carefully fold the fabric over itself so that the bias edges are even. Continue to cut the bias strips.

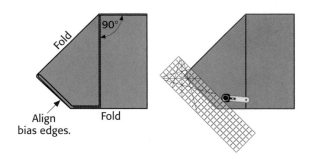

Align bias edges.

Follow these steps to bind the edges:

1. Cut 2¼"-wide bias strips as shown on page 29 and above.

2. Stitch the bias strips together, offsetting them as shown, to make one continuous strip. Press the seams open.

3. Press the strip in half lengthwise, wrong sides together.

4. Unfold the binding at one end and turn under ¼" at a 45° angle as shown.

5. Beginning on one side of the quilt, stitch the binding to the quilt, using a ¼"-wide seam allowance. Start stitching 1" to 2" from the start of the binding. Stop stitching ¼" from the corner and backstitch.

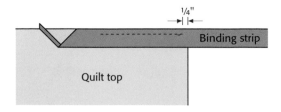

6. Turn the quilt to prepare for sewing along the next edge. Fold the binding away from the quilt as shown, and then fold again to place the binding along the second edge of the quilt. (This fold creates an angled pleat at the corner.)

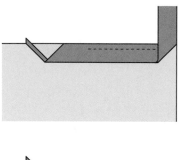

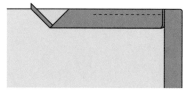

7. Stitch from the fold of the binding along the second edge of the quilt top, stopping ¼" from the corner as you did for the first corner; backstitch. Repeat the stitching and mitering process on the remaining edges and corners of the quilt.

8. When you reach the beginning of the binding, cut the end 1" longer than needed and tuck the end inside the beginning. Stitch the rest of the binding.

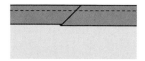

9. Turn the binding to the back of the quilt, over the raw edges, and blindstitch in place so that the folded edge covers the row of machine stitching. At each corner, fold the binding as shown to form a miter on the back of the quilt.

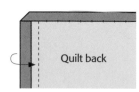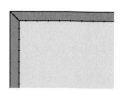

# QUILT LABELS

It's a good idea to label a quilt with its name, the name and address of the maker, and the date on which it was made. Include the name of the quilter(s) if the quilt was quilted by a group or someone other than the maker. On an antique quilt, record all the information you know about the quilt, including where you purchased it. If the quilt is being presented to someone as a gift, also include that information.

To easily make a label, use a permanent-ink pen to print or legibly write all this information on a piece of muslin. Press freezer paper to the back of the muslin to stabilize it while you write. Press raw edges to the wrong side of the label. Remove the freezer paper and stitch the label securely to a lower corner on the back of the quilt. You can also do labels in cross-stitch or embroidery.

# QUILT SLEEVES

If you plan to hang your quilt, attach a sleeve or rod pocket to the back before adding the binding. From the leftover backing fabric, cut an 8"-wide strip of fabric equal to the width of your quilt. You may need to piece two or three strips together for larger quilts. On each end, fold over ½" and then fold ½" again. Press and stitch by machine.

½"  ½"

Fold the strip in half lengthwise, wrong sides together; baste the raw edges to the top edge of the back of your quilt. These will be secured when you sew on the binding. Your quilt should be about 1" wider than the sleeve on both sides. Make a little pleat in the sleeve to accommodate the thickness of the rod, and then slipstitch the ends and bottom edge of the sleeve to the backing fabric. This keeps the rod from being inserted next to the quilt backing.

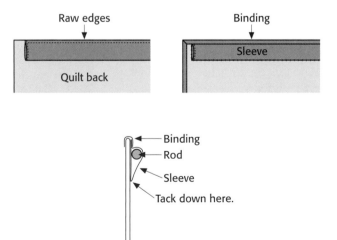

# Kansas Troubles

By Nancy J. Martin, Woodinville, Washington, 2003.

Quilted by Fannie Mae Petersheim, La Rue, Ohio.

Finished quilt size: 76" x 76"

Finished block size: 16" x 16"

Setting: 16 blocks set 4 across and 4 down;
1"-wide inner border; 5"-wide outer border

Kansas Troubles

# MATERIALS

*Yardage is based on 42"-wide fabric.*

2½ yards of red stripe fabric for outer border

½ yard *each* of 16 assorted light prints for blocks

½ yard *each* of 16 assorted dark prints for blocks

½ yard of dark red fabric for inner border

4½ yards of fabric for backing

1 yard of fabric for binding

Batting and thread to finish

Bias Square ruler to cut bias squares

# CUTTING

*All measurements include ¼"-wide seam allowances.*

**From *each* of the 16 assorted light prints, cut:**

2 squares, 8" x 8" (32 total)

2 squares, 8⅞" x 8⅞" (32 total); cut each square
in half once diagonally to yield 64 triangles

4 squares, 2½" x 2½" (64 total)

**From *each* of the 16 assorted dark prints, cut:**

2 squares, 8" x 8" (32 total)

2 squares, 4⅞" x 4⅞" (32 total); cut each square
in half once diagonally to yield 64 triangles

4 squares, 2⅞" x 2⅞" (64 total); cut each square
in half once diagonally to yield 128 triangles

**From the dark red fabric, cut:**

8 strips, 1½" x 42"

**From the red stripe fabric, cut:**

4 strips, 5¼" x 78", along the lengthwise grain.
Take care to cut the strips so the stripes will
line up at the mitered corners.

# INSTRUCTIONS

1. Pair each 8" light square with an 8" dark
   square, right sides up. Referring to "Basic
   Bias Square Technique" on page 16, cut and
   piece 2½"-wide strips, and then cut 256 bias
   squares, 2½" x 2½".

Cut 256.

2. Choosing fabrics randomly, join four bias
   squares, one 2½" light square, two small
   dark-print triangles, and one large dark-print
   triangle as shown.

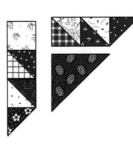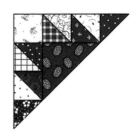

3. Join this unit to a large light-print triangle. Make 64 units.

Make 64.

4. Join four units as shown to make a block. Make 16.

Make 16.

5. Arrange and sew the blocks into four rows of four blocks each. Join the rows.

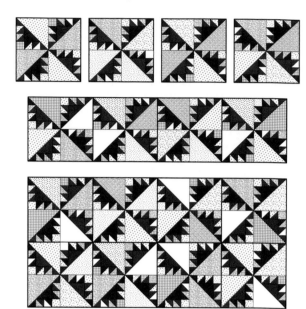

6. Refer to "Borders with Straight-Cut Corners" on page 23 to sew the 1½"-wide inner borders to the quilt top.

7. Refer to "Borders with Mitered Corners" on page 24 to sew the 5¼"-wide outer borders to the quilt top.

8. Mark the quilt top with the design of your choice. Layer with batting and backing; baste. Hand or machine quilt as desired.

9. Refer to "Binding the Edges" on page 29 to cut 2¼"-wide bias strips for binding. Make a total of 300" of bias binding and sew it to the quilt-top edges.

10. Make a label and attach it to the back of the quilt.

# Alternative Color Scheme

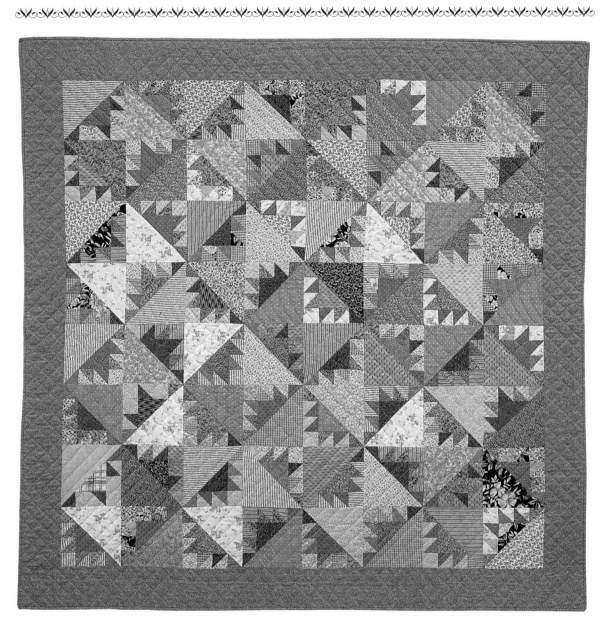

**Kansas Troubles** by Nancy J. Martin, Woodinville, Washington, 1991.

Quilted by Sue von Jentzen, Granite Falls, Washington.

Finished quilt size: 76" x 76"

Setting: 16 blocks set 4 across and 4 down; 6"-wide border.

Note that the blocks are set in a slightly different arrangement than the quilt on page 32.

# Keep the Shiny Side Up

By Julie Stewart, Kenmore, Washington, 2004.

Quilted by Susie Hostetler, La Rue, Ohio.

Owned by Quentin Stewart.

Finished quilt size: 74" x 90"

Finished block size: 8" x 8"

Setting: 63 blocks (32 block A, 31 block B) set
7 across and 9 down; 2"-wide inner border;
7"-wide outer border

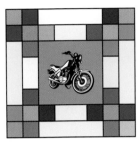 

Block A          Block B

## MATERIALS

*Yardage is based on 42"-wide fabric.*

3¼ yards of cream print for center of block B
and outer border

2½ yards *total* of assorted cream fabrics for
blocks

1⅝ yards *total* of assorted blue prints for blocks

½ yard *each* of 2 novelty prints for center of
block A

¾ yard *total* of assorted tan prints for blocks

¾ yard of blue fabric for inner border

5½ yards of fabric for backing

1 yard of fabric for binding

Batting and thread to finish

## CUTTING

*All measurements include ¼"-wide seam allowances.*

**From the assorted blue prints, cut a *total* of:**
30 strips, 1½" x 42"

**From the assorted tan prints, cut a *total* of:**
12 strips, 1½" x 42"

**From the assorted cream fabrics, cut a *total* of:**
3 strips, 4½" x 42"

6 strips, 2½" x 42"

3 strips, 6½" x 42"

62 rectangles, 1½" x 6½"

64 rectangles, 1½" x 4½"

**From *each* of the 2 novelty prints, cut:**
16 squares, 4½" x 4½" (32 total)

**From the cream print for block B center and
outer border, cut:**
2 strips, 7¼" x 78", along the lengthwise grain

2 strips, 7¼" x 76", along the lengthwise grain

31 squares, 6½" x 6½"

**From the blue fabric for inner border, cut:**
8 strips, 2½" x 42"

## BLOCK A

Refer to "Scrappy Strip Sets and Nine-Patch
Units" on page 15 to achieve a variety of prints
in the blocks.

1. Stitch two assorted tan and two assorted blue
   1½" x 42" strips and one assorted cream
   4½" x 42" strip together as shown to make
   strip set 1. Make three. Crosscut the strip sets
   into 64 segments, 1½" wide.

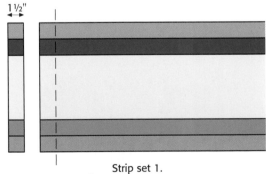

1½"

Strip set 1.
Make 3. Cut 64 segments.

2. Stitch two tan and four blue 1½" x 42" strips and one cream 2½" x 42" strip together as shown to make strip set 2. Make three. Crosscut the strip sets into 64 segments, 1½" wide.

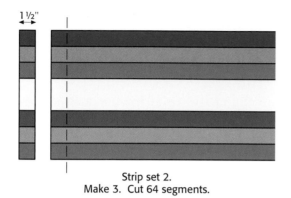

Strip set 2.
Make 3. Cut 64 segments.

3. Stitch two blue 1½" x 42" strips and one cream 2½" x 42" strip together as shown to make strip set 3. Make three. Crosscut the strip sets into 64 segments, 1½" wide.

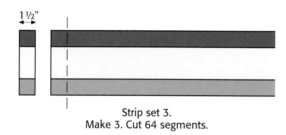

Strip set 3.
Make 3. Cut 64 segments.

4. Join the strip-set segments and assorted cream 1½" x 4½" rectangles to each novelty print square as shown. Make 32 blocks.

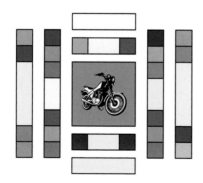

Make 32.

# BLOCK B

1. Stitch two blue 1½" x 42" strips and one cream 6½" x 42" strip together as shown to make strip set 4. Make three. Crosscut the strip sets into 62 segments, 1½" wide.

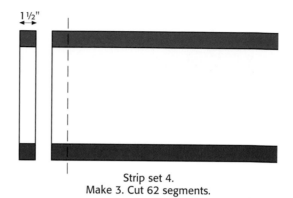

Strip set 4.
Make 3. Cut 62 segments.

2. Join the strip-set segments and the assorted cream 1½" x 6½" strips to each cream print square as shown. Make 31 blocks.

Make 31.

## ASSEMBLY

1. Refer to the diagram to arrange and sew the blocks into rows as shown, alternating the A and B blocks within each row and from row to row. Be careful to place each of the two novelty-print blocks in the positions shown. Join the rows.

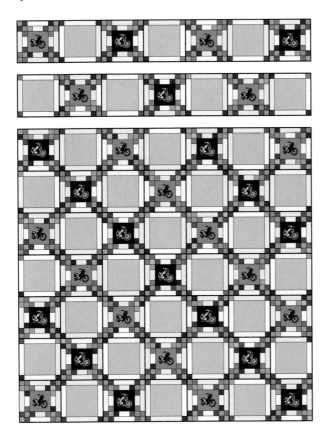

2. Refer to "Borders with Straight-Cut Corners" on page 23 to sew the 2½"-wide inner borders to the quilt top. Measure the quilt top for the outer borders. Trim the 7¼"-wide strips to the exact lengths needed and attach them to the quilt top in the same manner as the inner borders.

3. Mark the quilt top with the design of your choice. Layer with batting and backing; baste. Hand or machine quilt as desired.

4. Refer to "Binding the Edges" on page 29 to cut 2¼"-wide bias strips for binding. Make a total of 335" of bias binding and sew it to the quilt-top edges.

5. Make a label and attach it to the back of the quilt.

## Alternative Color Scheme

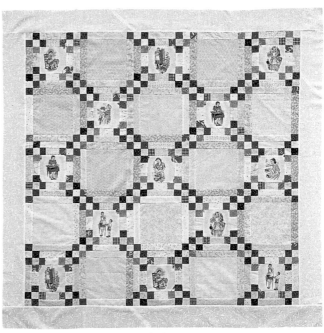

**Happy Housewife** by Nancy J. Martin, Kingston, Washington, 2005.

Finished quilt size: 46" x 46"

Setting: 25 blocks (13 block A, 12 block B) set 5 across and 5 down; 3"-wide border

# Memories of Provence

By Nancy J. Martin, Woodinville, Washington, 2002.
Quilted by Edna Borntreijor, La Rue, Ohio.

Finished quilt size: 81½" x 81½"

Finished block size: 12" x 12"

Setting: 13 blocks set diagonally; 1¼"-wide sashing and sashing squares; 10"-wide border

Memory Wreath

## MATERIALS

*Yardage is based on 42"-wide fabric.*

3½ yards of green fabric for border and binding

¾ yard *each* of 3 red fabrics for blocks and sashing squares

⅞ yard *each* of 2 light fabrics for background

1⅛ yards of red paisley border-print fabric for setting pieces

¾ yard of green fabric for sashing

3 fat quarters of assorted green fabrics for blocks

3 fat eighths of assorted yellow fabrics for blocks

4½ yards of fabric for backing

Batting and thread to finish

Bias Square ruler to cut bias squares

**Design Note:** Each block fabric is used in four blocks, with your favorite repeating in the "lucky 13th" block. Mix and match the two or three prints in each color family to create 13 different scrappy variations. Keep the fabric placement consistent within each block.

## CUTTING

*All measurements include ¼"-wide seam allowances.*

**From *each* of the 3 red fabrics, cut:**

2 squares, 8" x 8"; cut 1 extra square from your favorite red fabric (7 total)

8 squares, 3⅞" x 3⅞"; cut 2 extra squares from your favorite red fabric (26 total). Cut each square in half once diagonally to yield 52 triangles.

8 squares, 4¼" x 4¼"; cut 2 extra squares from your favorite red fabric (26 total). Cut each square in half twice diagonally to yield 104 triangles.

**From 1 of the remaining red fabrics, cut:**

24 squares, 1¾" x 1¾"

**From *each* of the 3 yellow fat eighths, cut:**

4 squares, 4¾" x 4¾"; cut 1 extra square from your favorite yellow fabric (13 total)

**Note:** Red center squares were intermixed with the yellow center squares in the photo shown on page 40, because I ran out of yellow fabric. However, I think this deviation from my fabric recipe adds spontaneity to the quilt.

**From *each* of the 2 light fabrics; cut:**

3 squares, 8" x 8"; cut 1 extra square from your favorite light fabric (7 total)

24 squares, 3½" x 3½"; cut 4 extra squares from your favorite light fabric (52 total)

12 squares, 4¼" x 4¼"; cut 2 extra squares from your favorite light fabric (26 total). Cut each square in half twice diagonally to yield 104 triangles.

**From *each* of the 3 green fat quarters, cut:**

8 squares, 4¼" x 4¼"; cut 2 extra squares from your favorite green fabric (26 total). Cut each square in half twice diagonally to yield 104 triangles.

**From the green fabric for sashing, cut:**

36 strips, 1¾" x 12½"

**From the red paisley border-print fabric, cut:**

2 squares, 21¾" x 21¾"; cut each square in half twice diagonally to yield 8 side setting triangles

2 squares, 11¼" x 11¼"; cut each square in half once diagonally to yield 4 corner setting triangles

**From the green fabric for border, cut:**

2 strips, 10¼" x 63", along the lengthwise grain

2 strips, 10¼" x 83", along the lengthwise grain

# INSTRUCTIONS

1. Pair each 8" light square with an 8" red square, right sides up. Referring to "Basic Bias Square Technique" on page 16, cut and piece 2½"-wide strips, and then cut 52 bias squares, 2⅝" x 2⅝".

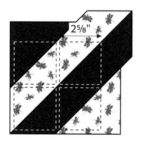 

Cut 52.

2. Join four matching red 3⅞" triangles to a 4¾" yellow square to make the center unit, joining opposite sides first.

Make 1.

3. Join one bias square, two matching light triangles, two matching red triangles, and two matching green triangles as shown to make a unit. Make four identical units.

Make 4.

4. Stitch two units from step 3 to the sides of the center unit as shown.

 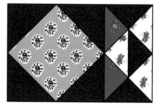

5. Join a 3½" light square to each end of the remaining two units from step 3. The squares should be from the same fabric.

Make 2.

6. Stitch the units from step 5 to the top and bottom of the center unit as shown to complete the block.

7. Repeat steps 2–6 to make 13 Memory Wreath blocks.

8. Arrange and join the blocks, sashing strips, red 1¾" squares, and side setting triangles into diagonal rows as shown. Press the seam allowances toward the sashing strips.

9. Join the sashing rows and block rows. Add a corner setting triangle to each corner of the quilt top. Press the seam allowances toward the sashing rows.

10. Refer to "Borders with Straight-Cut Corners" on page 23 to measure the quilt top for the border. Trim the 10¼"-wide strips to the exact lengths needed and attach them to the quilt top.

11. Mark the quilt top with the design of your choice. Layer with batting and backing; baste. Hand or machine quilt as desired.

12. Refer to "Binding the Edges" on page 29 to cut 2¼"-wide bias strips for binding. Make a total of 310" of bias binding and sew it to the quilt-top edges.

13. Make a label and attach it to the back of the quilt.

## Alternative Color Scheme

**Memory Wreath** by Nancy J. Martin, Woodinville, Washington, 2003. Quilted by Alvina Nelson, Salina, Kansas. Owned by Cleo Nollette.

Finished quilt size: 56½" x 56½"

Setting: 5 blocks set diagonally; 2"-wide sashing and sashing squares; 1"-wide inner border; 6"-wide outer border

# Crossed Kayaks

By Nancy J. Martin, Kingston, Washington, 2004.
Quilted by Fannie Schwartz, Seymour, Missouri.
Owned by Daniel J. Martin.

Finished quilt size: 72" x 72"

Finished block size: 12" x 12"

Setting: 16 blocks set 4 across and 4 down; 2"-wide sashing and sashing squares; 1"-wide inner border; 6"-wide outer border

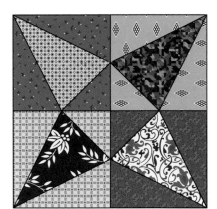

Crossed Kayaks

## MATERIALS

*Yardage is based on 42"-wide fabric.*

12 fat quarters of assorted light beige or cream fabrics for background

12 fat quarters of assorted dark brown, cranberry, and rust fabrics for background

2¼ yards of cranberry fabric for outer border

1⅛ yards of cranberry print fabric for sashing

½ yard of light print for inner border

¼ yard of rust check for sashing squares

4½ yards of fabric for backing

⅞ yard of fabric for binding

Batting and thread to finish

## CUTTING

*All measurements include ¼"-wide seam allowances. Templates are on page 47.*

**From the 12 light fat quarters, cut a *total* of:**
*For each 3⅞" square, cut two template 1, template 2, and template 2 reversed pieces from the same fabric.*

16 squares, 3⅞" x 3⅞"; cut each square in half once diagonally to yield 32 triangles

32 pieces from template 1

32 pieces from template 2

32 pieces from template 2 reversed

**From the 12 dark fat quarters, cut a *total* of:**
*For each 3⅞" square, cut two template 1, template 2, and template 2 reversed pieces from the same fabric.*

16 squares, 3⅞" x 3⅞"; cut each square in half once diagonally to yield 32 triangles

32 pieces from template 1

32 pieces from template 2

32 pieces from template 2 reversed

**From the cranberry print for sashing, cut:**
40 strips, 2½" x 12½"

**From the rust check, cut:**
25 squares, 2½" x 2½"

**From the light print for inner border, cut:**
8 strips, 1½" x 42"

**From the cranberry fabric for outer border, cut:**
2 strips, 6¼" x 62", along the lengthwise grain

2 strips, 6¼" x 74", along the lengthwise grain

## INSTRUCTIONS

1. Make 32 of unit 1 as shown using dark template 1 triangles and matching light template 2, template 2 reversed, and 3⅞" triangles.

Unit 1.
Make 32.

2. Make 32 of unit 2 as shown using light template 1 triangles and matching dark template 2, template 2 reversed, and 3⅞" triangles.

Unit 2.
Make 32.

3. Join two of unit 1 and two of unit 2 to make a block. Make 16 Crossed Kayak blocks.

Make 16.

4. Join four blocks and five sashing strips as shown to make a block row. Make four rows.

Make 4.

5. Join four sashing strips and five sashing squares as shown to make a sashing row. Make five rows.

Make 5.

6. Join the block rows and sashing rows as shown.

7. Refer to "Borders with Straight-Cut Corners" on page 23 to sew the 1½"-wide inner borders to the quilt top. Measure the quilt top for the outer borders. Trim the 6¼"-wide outer border strips to the exact lengths needed and attach them to the quilt top in the same manner as the inner borders.

8. Mark the quilt top with the design of your choice. Layer with batting and backing; baste. Hand or machine quilt as desired.

9. Refer to "Binding the Edges" on page 29 to cut 2¼"-wide bias strips for binding. Make a total of 300" of bias binding and sew it to the quilt-top edges.

10. Make a label and attach it to the back of the quilt.

# Alternative Color Scheme

**Crossed Kayaks** by Cleo Nollette, Seattle, Washington, 2004.
Quilted by Emma Miller, Navarre, Ohio.

Finished quilt size: 32" x 32"

Setting: 4 blocks set 2 across
and 2 down; 4"-wide border

**Triangle 1**
Cut 32 from light fat quarters.
Cut 32 from dark fat quarters.

Straight of grain

**Triangle 2**
Cut 32 and 32 reversed
from light fat quarters.
Cut 32 and 32 reversed
from dark fat quarters.

¼" seam allowance

# Chimneys and Cornerstones

By Nancy J. Martin, Woodinville, Washington, 1999.
Quilted by Elsie Mast, Charm, Ohio.

Finished quilt size: 66½" x 66½"

Finished block size: 11½" x 11½"

Setting: 25 blocks set 5 across and 5 down; 1½"-wide sashing and sashing squares

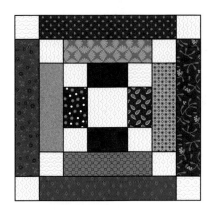

Chimneys and Cornerstones

## MATERIALS

*Yardage is based on 42"-wide fabric.*

1⅜ yards of light fabric for center squares and cornerstones

⅜ yard *each* of 8 assorted red prints for round 1 and sashing

⅜ yard *each* of 8 assorted navy prints for round 3

¼ yard *each* of 8 assorted tan or gold prints for round 2

4 yards of fabric for backing

⅞ yard of fabric for binding

Batting and thread to finish

## CUTTING

*All measurements include ¼"-wide seam allowances.*

### From the light fabric, cut:

2 strips, 3" x 42"; crosscut the strips into 25 squares, 3" x 3"

17 strips, 2" x 42"; crosscut the strips into 336 squares, 2" x 2"

### From *each* of the 8 assorted red prints, cut:

1 strip, 2" x 42"; crosscut the strip into 13 rectangles, 2" x 3" (104 total). You will use 100 and have 4 left over.

3 strips, 2" x 42"; crosscut the strips into 8 rectangles, 2" x 12" (64 total). You will use 60 and have 4 left over.

### From *each* of the 8 assorted tan or gold prints, cut:

3 strips, 2" x 42"; crosscut the strips into 13 rectangles, 2" x 6" (104 total). You will use 100 and have 4 left over.

### From *each* of the 8 assorted navy prints, cut:

4 strips, 2" x 42"; crosscut the strips into 13 rectangles, 2" x 9" (104 total). You will use 100 and have 4 left over.

## INSTRUCTIONS

1. Round 1: Using assorted fabrics, stitch a 2" x 3" red rectangle to the sides of each 3" light square. Stitch a 2" light square to the ends of each of the remaining 2" x 3" red rectangles and join these units to the top and bottom of each 3" light square.

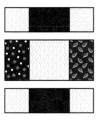

2. Round 2: Repeat step 1 with the 2" x 6" tan or gold rectangles.

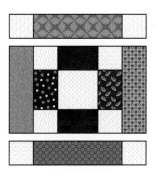

3. Round 3: Repeat step 1 with the 2" x 9" navy rectangles to complete a Chimneys and Cornerstones block. Make 25.

Make 25.

4. Join five blocks and six 2" x 12" red rectangles as shown to make a block row. Make five rows.

Make 5.

5. Join six 2" light squares and five 2" x 12" red rectangles as shown to make a sashing row. Make six rows.

Make 6.

6. Stitch the block rows and sashing rows together as shown.

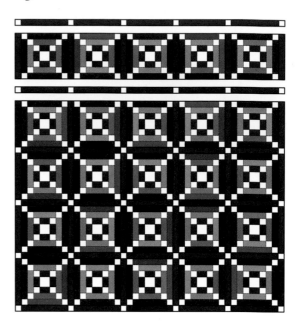

7. Mark the quilt top with the design of your choice. Layer with batting and backing; baste. Hand or machine quilt as desired.

8. Refer to "Binding the Edges" on page 29 to cut 2¼"-wide bias strips for binding. Make a total of 272" of bias binding and sew it to the quilt-top edges.

9. Make a label and attach it to the back of the quilt.

# Alternative Color Scheme

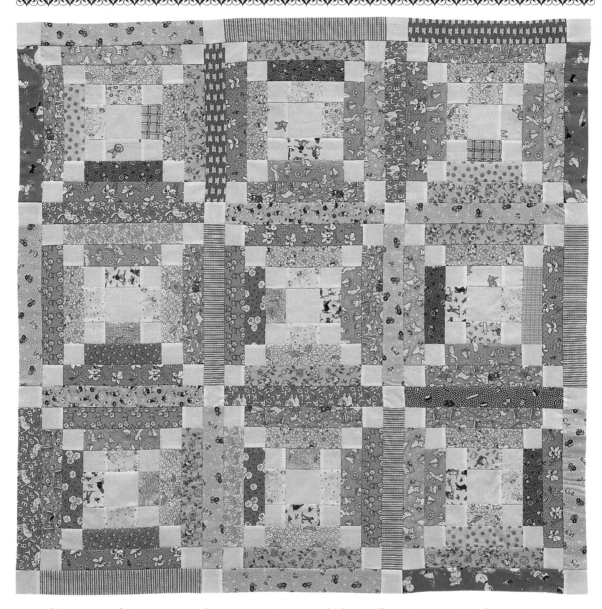

**Chimneys and Cornerstones** by Nancy J. Martin and Cleo Nollette, Kingston, Washington, 2005.

Finished quilt size: 37½" x 37½"

Setting: 9 blocks set 3 across and 3 down; 1½"-wide sashing and sashing squares

# Pot of Flowers

By Cleo Nollette and Nancy J. Martin, Kingston, Washington, 2004.
Quilted by Susie Hostetler, La Rue, Ohio.

Finished quilt size: 85" x 106"

Finished block size: 15" x 15"

Setting: 12 blocks, set diagonally,
3 across and 4 down with alternate plain blocks;
1¾"-wide inner border; 1"-wide middle border;
7¾"-wide outer border

Pot of Flowers

# MATERIALS

*Yardage is based on 42"-wide fabric.*

3 yards of yellow print for alternate blocks and
setting pieces

2⅞ yards of pink fabric for outer border

10 fat quarters of assorted light pink prints for
flowers

10 fat quarters of assorted medium pink prints
for flowers

6 fat quarters of assorted dark pink prints for pots

1 yard *each* of 3 assorted yellow prints for pieced
block backgrounds (You may use the alternate
block print as one of your choices.)

¾ yard of green print for stems and leaves

⅝ yard of green striped fabric for inner border

½ yard of yellow fabric for middle border

5½ yards of fabric for backing

1 yard of fabric for binding

½"-wide bias bar or Celtic bar for making stems

Batting and thread to finish

**Design Note:** This quilt uses the fabric-recipe
approach for scrap quilts. All of the pots are cut
from dark pink prints. Intermix the dark and medium prints for the flower tips. Use the medium and
light prints for the flower centers, making sure
there is a good contrast. All three flowers in each
pot are cut from different fabrics. The background
pieces within each block are all cut from the
same fabric; use each background fabric for four
blocks.

# CUTTING

*All measurements include ¼"-wide seam allowances.*

**From *each* of the 3 assorted yellow prints for
the pieced block backgrounds, cut:**

12 squares, 3½" x 3½" (36 total)

6 squares, 4¼" x 4¼" (18 total); cut each square
in half twice diagonally to yield 72 triangles

8 rectangles, 3½" x 6½" (24 total)

8 rectangles, 2" x 6½" (24 total)

2 squares, 3⅞" x 3⅞" (6 total); cut each square in
half once diagonally to yield 12 triangles

2 squares, 8⅜" x 8⅜" (6 total); cut each square in
half once diagonally to yield 12 triangles

**From *each* of the 6 assorted dark pink
prints, cut:**

1 square, 8⅜" x 8⅜" (6 total); cut each square in
half once diagonally to yield 12 triangles

2 squares, 2⅜" x 2⅜" (12 total); cut each square
in half once diagonally to yield 24 triangles

**From the assorted medium and dark pink
prints, cut a *total* of:**

36 squares, 4¼" x 4¼"; cut each square in half
twice diagonally to yield 144 triangles

**From the assorted medium and light pink
prints, cut a *total* of:**

18 squares, 4¼" x 4¼"; cut each square in half
twice diagonally to yield 72 triangles

36 squares, 3½" x 3½"

**From the yellow print for alternate blocks and setting pieces, cut:**

3 squares, 22½" x 22½"; cut each square in half twice diagonally to yield 12 side setting triangles. You will use 10 and have 2 left over.

6 squares, 15½" x 15½"

2 squares, 11½" x 11½"; cut each square in half once diagonally to yield 4 corner setting triangles

**From the green striped fabric, cut:**

8 strips, 2¼" x 42"

**From the yellow fabric for middle border, cut:**

9 strips, 1½" x 42"

**From the pink fabric for outer border, cut:**

2 strips, 8¼" x 92", along the lengthwise grain

2 strips, 8¼" x 86", along the lengthwise grain

# INSTRUCTIONS

1. Join one background 4¼" triangle, two matching medium or dark 4¼" triangles, and one medium or light 4¼" triangle as shown to make the flower-tip units. Make 36 pairs.

Make 36 pairs.

2. Make the basket unit as shown, using one 8⅜" triangle and two 2⅜" triangles from the same dark pink fabric, and one 8⅜" triangle, one 3⅞" triangle, and two 2" x 6½" rectangles from the same background fabric. Make 12.

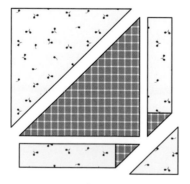

Make 12.

3. Piece 12 Pot of Flowers blocks as shown, by using three different pairs of flower-tip units, three yellow 3½" squares, two pink 3½" squares, two yellow 3½" x 6½" rectangles, and one basket unit.

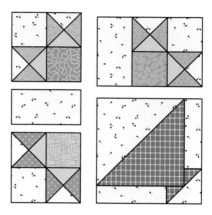

Make 12.

4. Referring to "Appliqué" on page 21, use the green fabric and the pattern on page 55 to make 48 leaf shapes. Refer to "Bias Stems" on page 22 to cut the remaining green print fabric into 1¼"-wide bias strips and make bias tubes for the stems. Cut the bias tubes to the desired lengths for the stems. Appliqué three stems and four leaves to each block. Open previously sewn seams along the basket top to insert the raw edges of the stem pieces. Resew these seams after the appliqué is completed.

Make 12.

5. Stitch the completed blocks, the alternate blocks, and the setting pieces into diagonal rows as shown. Stitch the rows together.

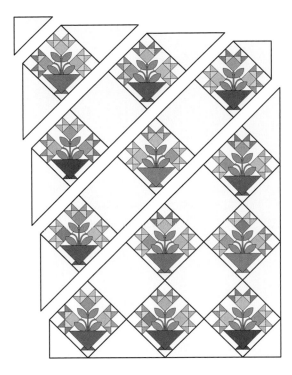

6. Refer to "Borders with Straight-Cut Corners" on page 23 to sew the 2¼"-wide inner borders to the quilt top. Repeat for the 1½"-wide middle borders. Measure the quilt top for the outer borders. Trim the 8¼"-wide outer borders to the exact lengths needed and attach them to the quilt top in the same manner as the inner and middle borders.

7. Mark the quilt top with the design of your choice. Layer with batting and backing; baste. Hand or machine quilt as desired.

8. Refer to "Binding the Edges" on page 29 to cut 2¼"-wide bias strips for binding. Make a total of 472" of bias binding and sew it to the quilt-top edges.

9. Make a label and attach it to the back of the quilt.

## Alternative Color Scheme

**Pot of Flowers Pillow** by Cleo Nollete, Seattle, Washington, 2005.

Finished pillow size: 21" x 22"

Setting: 1 block set diagonally with corner triangles

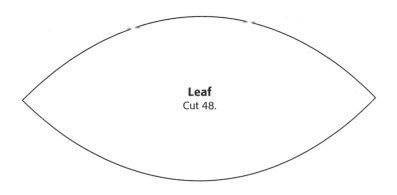

**Leaf**
Cut 48.

# Sawtooth Medallion

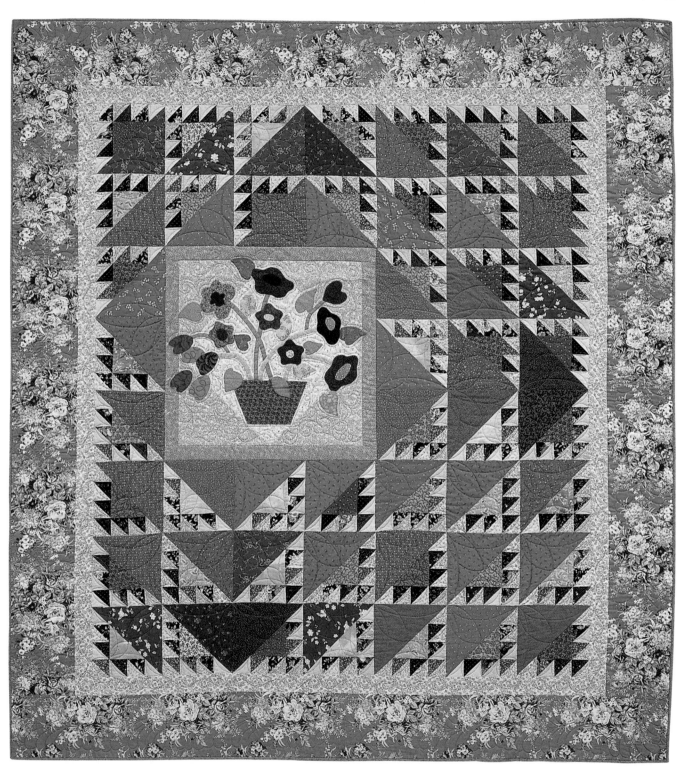

**Overcoming Our Troubles** by Mary Hickey, Everett, Washington, 2002.
Quilted by Fannie Schwartz, Seymour, Missouri.

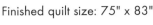

Finished quilt size: 75" x 83"

Finished block size: 8" x 8"

Setting: 24" framed medallion set off-center, surrounded by 47 blocks set 7 across and 8 down; 2"-wide inner border; 7½"-wide outer border

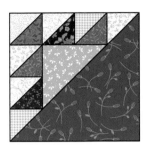

Sawtooth

# MATERIALS

*Yardage is based on 42"-wide fabric.*

2⅝ yards of floral print for outer border

2⅜ yards *total* of assorted light pink prints for medallion background and blocks

2 yards *total* of assorted dark blue prints for blocks and appliqués

2 yards *total* of assorted medium blue prints for blocks and appliqués

¾ yard *total* of assorted medium pink prints for blocks

⅝ yard of light blue print for medallion background

⅝ yard of light pink print for inner border

⅜ yard of light blue print for medallion border

¼ yard *each* of 3 assorted green prints for appliqué

¼ yard *each* of 6 assorted rose prints for appliqué

5½ yards of fabric for backing

1 yard of fabric for binding

Batting and thread to finish

Bias Square ruler to cut bias squares

½"-wide bias bar or Celtic bar for making stems

# CUTTING

*All measurements include ¼"-wide seam allowances.*

**From the assorted light pink prints for medallion background and blocks, cut a *total* of:**

2 squares, 10⅞" x 10⅞"; cut each square in half once diagonally to yield 4 large triangles

30 squares, 8" x 8"

47 squares, 2⅞" x 2⅞"; cut each square in half once diagonally to yield 94 small triangles

**From the assorted dark blue prints, cut a *total* of:**

30 squares, 8" x 8"

**From the assorted medium pink prints, cut a *total* of:**

24 squares, 4⅞" x 4⅞"; cut each square in half once diagonally to yield 48 triangles. You will use 47 and have 1 left over.

**From the assorted medium blue prints, cut a *total* of:**

24 squares, 8⅞" x 8⅞"; cut each square in half once diagonally to yield 48 triangles. You will use 47 and have 1 left over.

**From the light blue print for medallion background, cut:**

1 square, 14⅝" x 14⅝"

**From the light blue print for medallion border, cut:**

3 strips, 2½" x 42"

**From the light pink print for inner border, cut:**

7 strips, 2½" x 42"

**From the floral print, cut:**

2 strips, 7¾" x 70", along the lengthwise grain

2 strips, 7¾" x 77", along the lengthwise grain

# INSTRUCTIONS

1. Pair each 8" light pink square with an 8" dark blue square, right sides up. Referring to "Basic Bias Square Technique" on page 16, cut and piece 2½"-wide strips, and then cut 235 bias squares, 2½" x 2½".

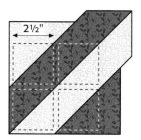

Cut 235.

2. Choosing fabrics randomly, join five bias squares, two small light pink triangles, and one medium pink triangle as shown to form a unit. Make 47.

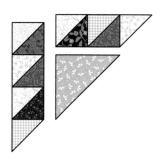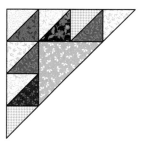

Make 47.

3. Stitch a medium blue triangle to each unit to make a Sawtooth block. Make 47.

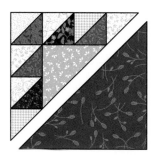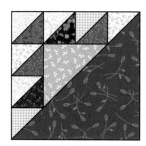

Make 47.

4. To make the medallion, stitch the large light pink triangles to the sides of the light blue square, joining opposite sides first. Referring to "Borders with Straight-Cut Corners" on page 23, stitch the light blue strips to the sides of the square. Refer to "Appliqué" on page 21 to cut out the appliqué shapes on pages 61–63 from the appropriate fabrics as indicated on the patterns. Refer to "Bias Stems" on page 22 to cut the remainder of the green fabrics into 1¼"-wide bias strips and make bias tubes for the stems. Appliqué the pieces to the background as shown.

Appliqué placement

5. Arrange the blocks for rows 1 and 2 as shown, being careful to orient the blocks in the correct direction. Stitch the blocks in each row together and then stitch the rows together.

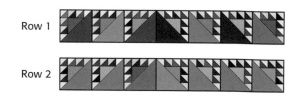

Row 1

Row 2

6. Arrange the blocks for the left side of rows 3, 4, and 5 as shown. Stitch the blocks together. Join the partial rows to the left side of the appliquéd medallion.

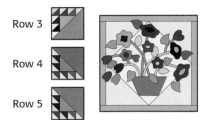

7. Arrange the blocks for the right side of rows 3, 4, and 5 as shown. Stitch the blocks in each row together and then stitch the rows together. Join the partial rows to the right side of the appliquéd medallion.

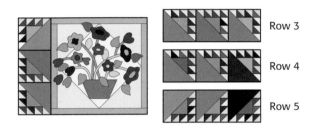

8. Arrange the blocks for rows 6, 7, and 8 as shown. Stitch the blocks in each row together and then stitch the rows together.

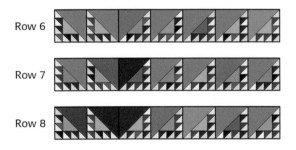

9. Join the sections of rows to form the completed quilt top.

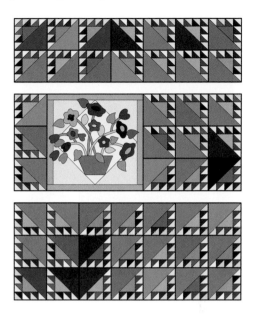

10. Refer to "Borders with Straight-Cut Corners" on page 23 to sew the 2½"-wide light pink strips to the quilt top. Measure the quilt top for the outer borders. Trim the 7¾"-wide floral strips to the exact lengths needed and attach them to the quilt top in the same manner as the inner border.

11. Mark the quilt top with the design of your choice. Layer with batting and backing; baste. Hand or machine quilt as desired.

12. Refer to "Binding the Edges" on page 29 to cut 2¼"-wide bias strips for binding. Make a total of 325" of bias binding and sew it to the quilt-top edges.

13. Make a label and attach it to the back of the quilt.

# Alternative Color Scheme

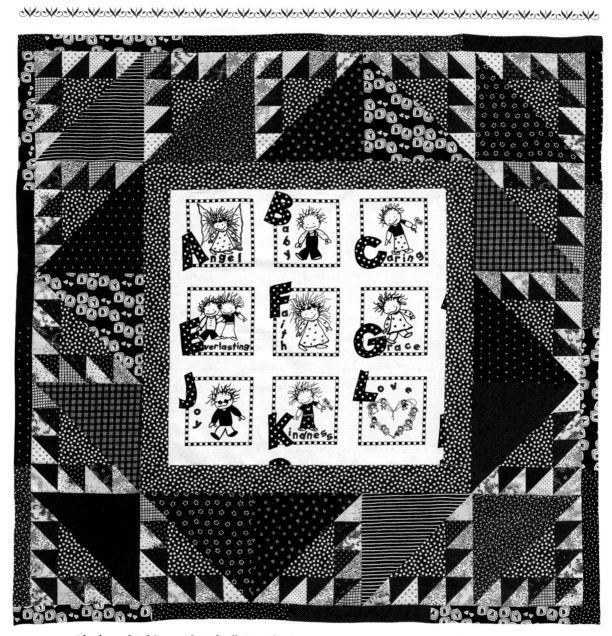

**Black and White and Red All Over** by Nancy J. Martin, Kingston, Washington, 2005.

Finished quilt size: 42" x 42"

Setting: 20" printed panel with 2"-wide border surrounded by
16 blocks set 5 across and 5 down; 1"-wide border

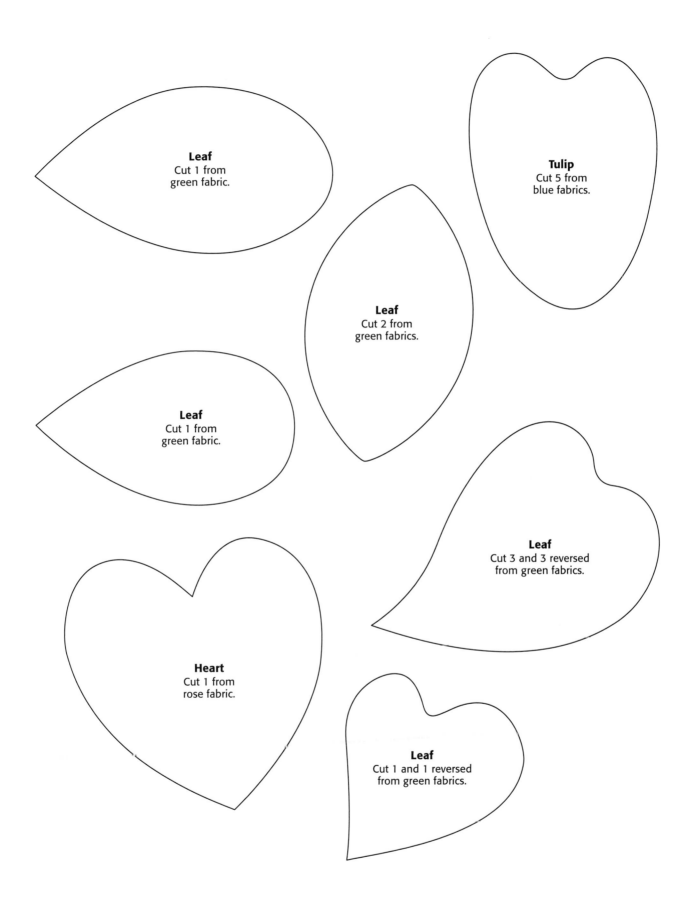

**Leaf**
Cut 1 from
green fabric.

**Tulip**
Cut 5 from
blue fabrics.

**Leaf**
Cut 2 from
green fabrics.

**Leaf**
Cut 1 from
green fabric.

**Leaf**
Cut 3 and 3 reversed
from green fabrics.

**Heart**
Cut 1 from
rose fabric.

**Leaf**
Cut 1 and 1 reversed
from green fabrics.

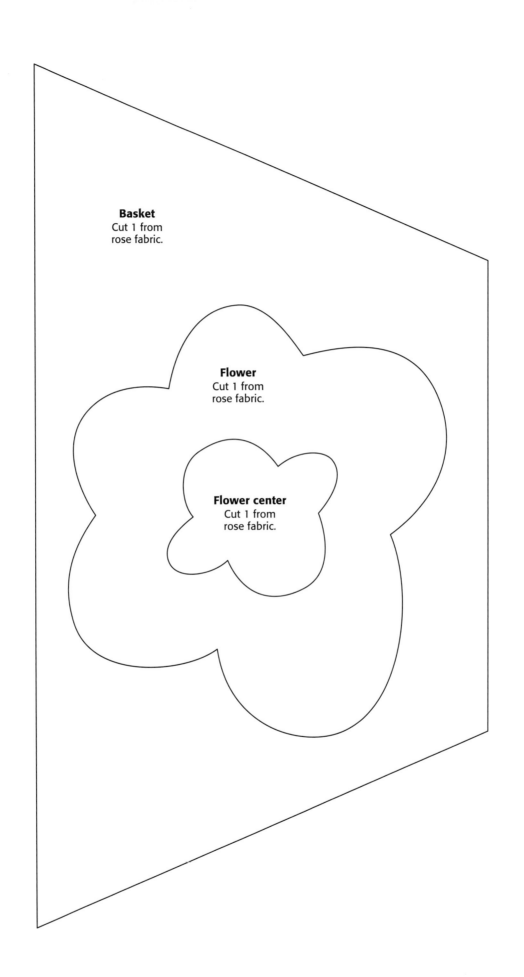

**Basket**
Cut 1 from
rose fabric.

**Flower**
Cut 1 from
rose fabric.

**Flower center**
Cut 1 from
rose fabric.

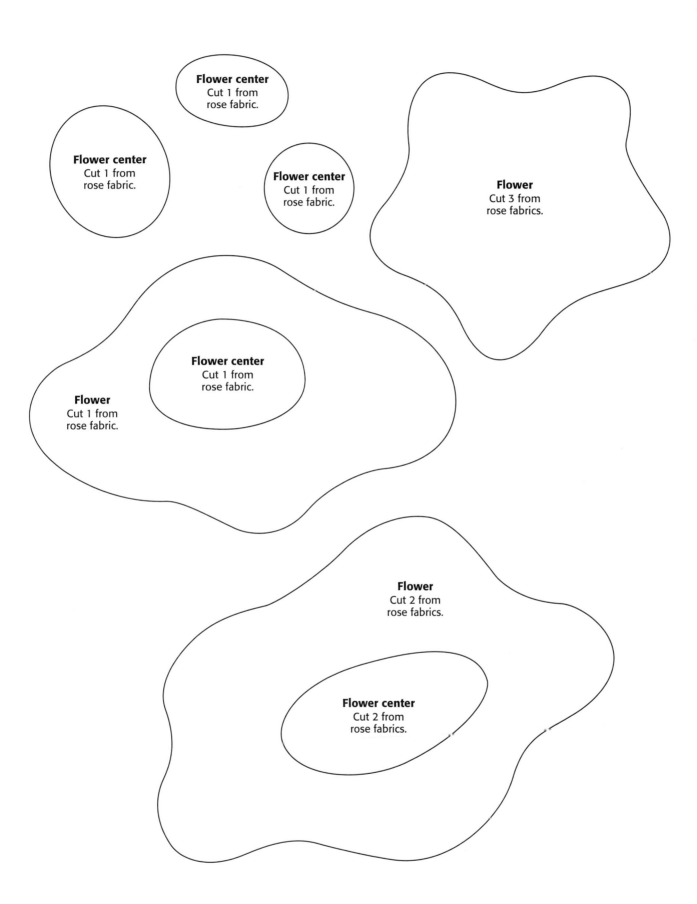

**Flower center**
Cut 1 from
rose fabric.

**Flower center**
Cut 1 from
rose fabric.

**Flower center**
Cut 1 from
rose fabric.

**Flower**
Cut 3 from
rose fabrics.

**Flower center**
Cut 1 from
rose fabric.

**Flower**
Cut 1 from
rose fabric.

**Flower**
Cut 2 from
rose fabrics.

**Flower center**
Cut 2 from
rose fabrics.

# Megan's Valentine Quilt

By Nancy J. Martin, Woodinville, Washington, 2003.

Quilted by Emma Miller, Navarre, Ohio.

Owned by Megan Jane Martin.

Finished quilt size: 62" x 82"

Finished block size: 10" x 10"

Setting: 35 blocks (18 block A, 17 block B) set 5 across and 7 down; 6"-wide pieced border

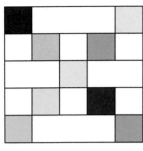

Block A

Block B

# MATERIALS

*Yardage is based on 42"-wide fabric.*

2 yards of novelty print fabric*

3 fat quarters *each* of assorted pink, blue, red, yellow, and green fabrics for blocks and border

3 yards *total* of assorted light prints for block backgrounds

5¼ yards of fabric for backing

1 yard of red fabric for binding

Batting and thread to finish

*\*Yardage may vary depending on the space between motifs. See page 14 for suggestions on cutting and spacing when using novelty prints. You can vary the size of the novelty print square by enlarging or reducing the surrounding strips.*

# CUTTING

*All measurements include ¼"-wide seam allowances.*

**From *each* of the 3 pink, blue, red, yellow, and green fat quarters, cut:**

38 squares, 2½" x 2½" (570 total); you will use 558 and have 12 left over

**From the assorted light prints, cut a *total* of:**

108 squares, 2½" x 2½"

36 rectangles, 2½" x 4½"

36 rectangles, 2½" x 6½"

34 strips, 2¼" x 7"

34 strips, 2¼" x 10½"

**From the novelty print fabric, cut:**

17 squares, 7" x 7"

# INSTRUCTIONS

1.  To make block A, arrange nine assorted 2½" pink, blue, yellow, and green squares; six 2½" light background squares; two 2½" x 4½" light print rectangles; and two 2½" x 6½" light print rectangles into five rows as shown. Stitch the pieces in each row together. Press the seams away from the light pieces. Stitch the rows together, being careful to match the seams. Make 18.

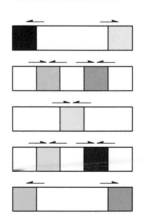

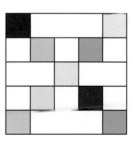

Make 18.

2. To make block B, join a 2¼" x 7" light print strip to opposite sides of a novelty print square. Join a 2¼" x 10½" light print strip to the top and bottom of the square. Make 17.

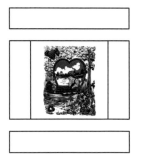

Make 17.

3. Arrange blocks A and B alternately in seven horizontal rows of five blocks each. Odd-numbered rows begin with pieced blocks; even-numbered rows begin with novelty print blocks. Sew the blocks in each row together and then sew the rows together to form the quilt top.

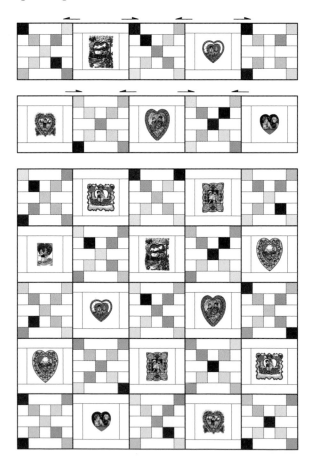

4. Randomly arrange 35 of the remaining 2½" pink, blue, red, yellow, and green squares to make a horizontal row. Sew the squares together, and press the seams in one direction. Make six rows.

Make 6.

5. Carefully sew three rows together along their long edges, matching the seams. Press the seams in one direction. Make two border units. Sew the units to the sides of the quilt top. Press the seams toward the borders.

6. Randomly arrange 31 of the remaining 2½" squares to make a horizontal row. Sew the squares together, and press the seams in one direction. Make six rows.

7. Repeat step 5 to make two border units of three rows each. Sew the units to the top and bottom edges of the quilt top. Press the seams toward the borders.

8. Mark the quilt top with the design of your choice. Layer with batting and backing; baste. Hand or machine quilt as desired.

9. Refer to "Binding the Edges" on page 29 to cut 2¼"-wide bias strips for binding. Make a total of 300" of bias binding and sew it to the quilt-top edges.

10. Make a label and attach it to the back of the quilt.

The back of the quilt hides fabric valentines from Nana, each one tucked into a pretty handkerchief envelope.

# Alternative Color Scheme

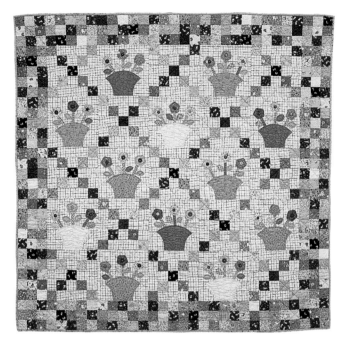

**Posy Pots** by Nancy J. Martin,
Woodinville, Washington, 2000.
Quilted by Rose Schwartz, Hillsdale, Michigan.

Finished quilt size: 62" x 62"

Setting: 25 blocks (13 block A, 12 block B)
set 5 across and 5 down; 6"-wide pieced border

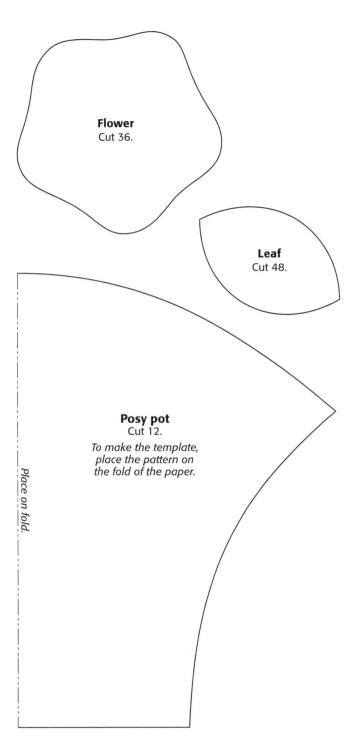

**Flower**
Cut 36.

**Leaf**
Cut 48.

**Posy pot**
Cut 12.

*To make the template,
place the pattern on
the fold of the paper.*

*Place on fold.*

# Barrister's Block

By Nancy J. Martin, Woodinville, Washington, 2004.
Quilted by Fannie Schwartz, Seymour, Missouri.
Owned by Margaret Philip.

Finished quilt size: 60" x 60"

Finished block size: 16" x 16"

Setting: 9 blocks set 3 across and 3 down;
4"-wide inner border; 2"-wide pieced outer border

Barrister's Block

# MATERIALS

*Yardage is based on 42"-wide fabric.*

¼ yard *each* of 18 assorted light prints for blocks*

¼ yard *each* of 18 assorted dark prints for blocks*

2 yards of dark blue print for inner border and
pieced outer border

⅝ yard of rust print for pieced outer border

3⅝ yards of fabric for backing

⅞ yard of fabric for binding

Batting and thread to finish

Bias Square ruler to cut bias squares

*Select a wide variety of stripes, checks, plaids,
shirtings, and patriotic prints with both light and
dark backgrounds.*

# CUTTING

*All measurements include ¼"-wide seam allowances.*

**From *each* of the 18 assorted light prints, cut:**

1 square, 8" x 8"; cut 1 additional square from 9
   fabrics (27 total)

1 square, 6⅞" x 6⅞" (18 total); cut each square in
   half once diagonally to yield 36 triangles

2 squares, 2½" x 2½" (36 total)

**From *each* of the 18 assorted dark prints, cut:**

1 square, 8" x 8"; cut 1 additional square from 9
   fabrics (27 total)

1 square, 6⅞" x 6⅞" (18 total); cut each square in
   half once diagonally to yield 36 triangles

**From the dark blue print, cut:**

2 strips, 4½" x 50", along the lengthwise grain

2 strips, 4½" x 58", along the lengthwise grain

14 squares, 5¼" x 5¼"; cut each square in half
   twice diagonally to yield 56 triangles

2 squares, 6¾" x 6¾"; cut each square in half
   once diagonally to yield 4 triangles

**From the rust print, cut:**

15 squares, 5¼" x 5¼"; cut each square in half
   twice diagonally to yield 60 triangles

# INSTRUCTIONS

1.  Pair each 8" light print square with an 8"
    dark print square, right sides up. Referring to
    "Basic Bias Square Technique" on page 16,
    cut and piece 2½"-wide strips, and then cut
    216 bias squares, 2½" x 2½".

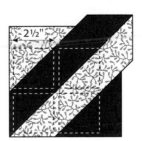

Cut 216.

2. Sew each 6⅞" dark triangle to a 6⅞" light triangle.

Make 36.

3. Choosing fabrics randomly, join six bias squares, one 2½" light square, and one pieced-triangle square from step 2 to make a unit. Make 36.

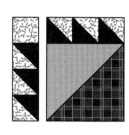

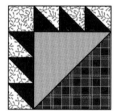

Make 36.

4. Stitch four units together as shown to make a Barrister's block. Make nine.

Make 9.

5. Arrange and sew the blocks into three rows of three blocks each as shown, being careful to keep the blocks oriented in the same direction.

6. Using the pattern on page 71 and referring to "Appliqué" on page 21, cut out 17 stars from the remainder of the light and dark fabrics. Randomly place six stars on the quilt top and appliqué them in place. Set the remaining stars aside for the border.

7. Refer to "Borders with Mitered Corners" on page 24 to stitch the 4½"-wide borders to the sides and top and bottom edges of the quilt top. Appliqué three stars in each corner of the border.

8. Join 14 dark blue 5¼" triangles and 15 rust 5¼" triangles to make an outer border strip. Make four.

Make 4.

9. With the dark blue triangles positioned next to the inner border, sew the pieced borders to the quilt top and miter the corners as for the inner border.

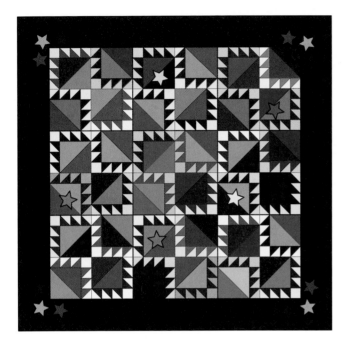

10. Mark the quilt top with the design of your choice. Layer with batting and backing; baste. Hand or machine quilt as desired.

11. Refer to "Binding the Edges" on page 29 to cut 2¼"-wide bias strips for binding. Make a total of 250" of bias binding and sew it to the quilt-top edges.

12. Make a label and attach it to the back of the quilt.

## Alternative Color Scheme

**Barrister's Block** by Nancy J. Martin, Woodinville, Washington, 2004.
Quilted by Emma Miller, Navarre, Ohio.

Finished quilt size: 40" x 40"

Setting: 4 blocks set 2 across and 2 down; 4"-wide border

**Star**
Cut 17.

# Orange Peel

By Nancy J. Martin and Cleo Nollette, Kingston, Washington, 2004.
Quilted by Treva Mast, Kenton, Ohio.

Finished quilt size: 53¼" x 53¼"

Finished block size: 9" x 9"

Setting: 13 blocks, framed with curved seams, set diagonally, with framed side and corner setting triangles; 1½"-wide inner border; 6"-wide outer border

Orange Peel

## MATERIALS

*Yardage is based on 42"-wide fabric.*

2⅜ yards of rose print fabric for outer border and binding

9 fat quarters of assorted rose fabrics

1⅛ yards of yellow tone-on-tone fabric

⅞ yard of yellow print fabric

⅜ yard of rose print fabric for inner border

3½ yards of fabric for backing

Batting and thread to finish

## CUTTING

*All measurements include ¼"-wide seam allowances. Templates are on pages 75 and 76.*

**From *each* of the 9 rose fat quarters, cut:**
8 pieces from template 2 (72 total)

**From the yellow print fabric, cut:**
8 pieces from template 3

2 pieces from template 4

1 piece from template 1

**From the yellow tone-on-tone fabric, cut:**
5 pieces from template 3

6 pieces from template 4

3 pieces from template 1

**From the rose print fabric for inner border, cut:**
4 strips, 2" x 42"

**From the rose print fabric for outer border, cut:**
2 strips, 6¼" x 43", along the lengthwise grain

2 strips, 6¼" x 55", along the lengthwise grain

## INSTRUCTIONS

1. Refer to "Tips for Curved Piecing" on page 74 to join four assorted template 3 pieces to each template 2 piece. Make nine Orange Peel blocks.

Make 9.

2. Join two template 2 pieces to each template 4 piece as shown, following the same tips. Make eight side setting pieces.

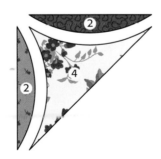 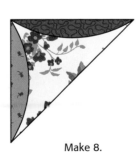

Make 8.

3. Join one template 2 piece to each template 1 piece, following the same tips. Make four corner setting pieces.

Make 4.

4. Arrange and join the Orange Peel blocks and side setting triangles into five diagonal rows as shown. Stitch the pieces in each row together. Press the seams open so they lie flat. This reduces bulk and makes it easier to match seams when stitching rows together. Stitch the rows together, matching seams. Add the corner setting triangles.

5. Refer to "Borders with Straight-Cut Corners" on page 23 to stitch the 2"-wide inner border strips to the quilt top. Measure the quilt top for the outer borders. Trim the 6¼"-wide outer border strips to the exact lengths needed and attach them to the quilt top in the same manner as the inner borders.

6. Mark the quilt top with the design of your choice. Layer with batting and backing; baste. Hand or machine quilt as desired.

7. Refer to "Binding the Edges" on page 29 to cut 2¼"-wide bias strips for binding. Make a total of 225" of bias binding and sew it to the quilt-top edges.

8. Make a label and attach it to the back of the quilt.

## TIPS FOR CURVED PIECING

1. Template 3 has concave curves and may need to be clipped to fit. Make ¹⁄₁₆" clips with the tips of your scissors about ¼" apart along the curved edges. If your fabric has a lot of stretch, you may not need to clip the curves.

2. Mark the center of both the convex and concave curves with a pin.

3. Pin the pieces together at the centers and at the beginning and end of each piece.

4. Stitch the curved seam with the concave piece on the top. Stitch slowly, taking only a few stitches at a time. Stop often to make sure that you're not sewing a pleat into the seam.

5. The seam may be pressed in either direction to lie flat; I always press toward the darker fabric.

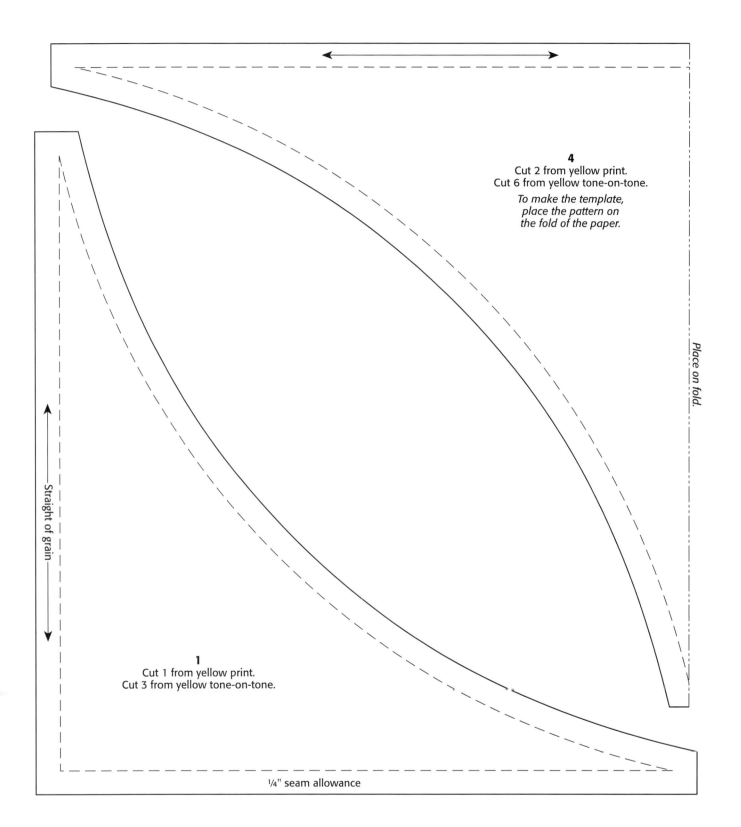

**4**
Cut 2 from yellow print.
Cut 6 from yellow tone-on-tone.

*To make the template,
place the pattern on
the fold of the paper.*

Place on fold.

Straight of grain

**1**
Cut 1 from yellow print.
Cut 3 from yellow tone-on-tone.

¼" seam allowance

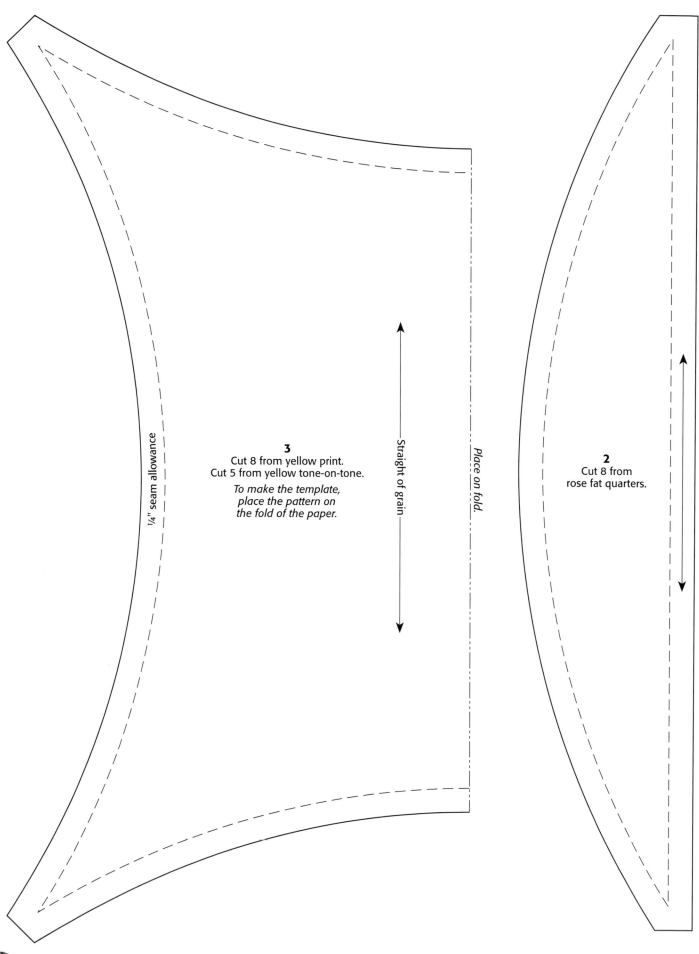

**3**
Cut 8 from yellow print.
Cut 5 from yellow tone-on-tone.

*To make the template,
place the pattern on
the fold of the paper.*

Straight of grain

Place on fold.

¼" seam allowance

**2**
Cut 8 from
rose fat quarters.

# Alternative Color Scheme

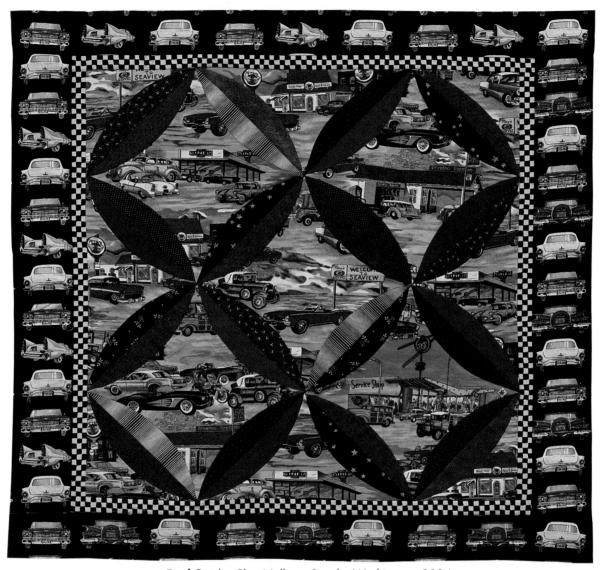

**Peel Out** by Cleo Nollette, Seattle, Washington, 2004.

Finished quilt size: 37½" x 37½"

Setting: 5 blocks, framed with curved seams, set diagonally, 2 across and 2 down,
with framed side and corner setting triangles; 2"-wide inner border; 4"-wide outer border

# Double Nine Patch

By Nancy J. Martin and Cleo Nollette, Woodinville, Washington, 2003.
Quilted by Anna Stutzman, Mount Victory, Ohio.
Owned by Laurel Strand.

Finished quilt size: 85" x 103"

Finished block size: 9" x 9"

Setting: 63 blocks, set 7 across and 9 down,
alternating the Double Nine Patch and Nine Patch blocks;
1"-wide inner border; 10"-wide outer border

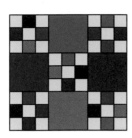 

Double Nine Patch          Nine Patch

## MATERIALS

*Yardage is based on 42"-wide fabric.*

3⅝ yards of fabric for outer border and binding

½ yard *each* of 6 assorted blue fabrics for blocks

2¼ yards of light blue fabric for Double Nine
Patch blocks and inner border

6 fat quarters of assorted turquoise fabrics for
blocks

6 fat quarters of assorted purple fabrics for
blocks

7½ yards of fabric for backing

Batting and thread to finish

**Design Note:** This jewel-tone quilt was made by prearranging the fabric pieces on a design wall to ensure that the colors would gradate diagonally from purple to blue to turquoise.

To make a design wall, purchase a large sheet of stable needle-punch batting and tack it to a wall. Fabric pieces will adhere to its surface without pinning, allowing them to be easily rearranged.

The small nine-patch units used in the Double Nine Patch blocks can be strip pieced, but it is best not to strip piece the Nine Patch blocks so that you can arrange them on the design wall before sewing them together. The cutting instructions allow for extra squares so that you will have plenty of choices as the colors change.

Also, don't be afraid to break the chain. In the lower-left corner, additional design interest was created by breaking the even rhythm of the chain.

## CUTTING

*All measurements include ¼"-wide seam allowances.*

**From the light blue fabric, cut:**
44 strips, 1½" x 42"; cut 18 strips in half crosswise to yield 36 strips, 1½" x 21". (You'll be
left with 26 strips measuring 42" long.)

**From the assorted purple fat quarters, cut a
*total* of:**
15 strips, 1½" x 21"
99 squares, 3½" x 3½"

**From the assorted turquoise fat quarters, cut
a *total* of:**
15 strips, 1½" x 21"
99 squares, 3½" x 3½"

**From the assorted blue fabrics, cut a *total* of:**

15 strips, 1½" x 42"

220 squares, 3½" x 3½"

**From the outer border fabric, cut:**

2 strips, 10¼" x 85", along the lengthwise grain

2 strips, 10¼" x 87", along the lengthwise grain

# INSTRUCTIONS

1. Make 170 nine-patch units for the Double Nine Patch blocks, referring to "Scrappy Strip Sets and Nine-Patch Units" on page 15. Using 1½" x 21" strips, make 45 *each* of predominantly purple units with a light blue chain and predominantly turquoise units with a light blue chain. Using 1½" x 42" strips, make 80 predominantly blue units with a light blue chain. These amounts will give you more units than required so you can play with the placement along the color breaks.

| Make 45. | Make 45. | Make 80. |

2. Arrange the nine-patch units on a design wall, placing colors as suggested in the design note.

3. Place 3½" squares on the design wall to complete the Double Nine Patch blocks. Arrange the remaining 3½" squares for the alternating Nine Patch blocks.

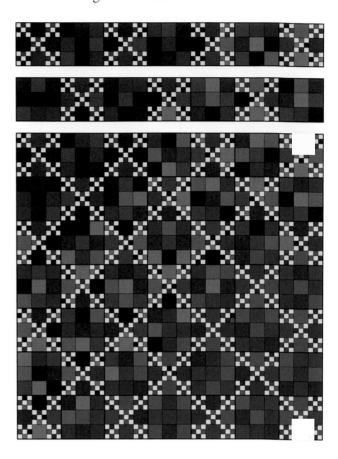

4. When you're satisfied with the arrangement, stitch the Double Nine Patch blocks to-gether, carefully removing the pieces for each block and then replacing the finished block on the design wall. Repeat with the Nine Patch blocks.

5. Join the blocks in each row. Stitch the rows together to complete the quilt top.

6. For the inner border, refer to "Borders with Straight-Cut Corners" on page 23 and add 1½"-wide blue strips to the quilt top. Then measure the quilt top for the outer borders. Trim the 10¼"-wide outer border strips to the exact lengths needed and attach them to the quilt top in the same manner as the inner border.

7. Mark the quilt top with the design of your choice. Layer with batting and backing; baste. Hand or machine quilt as desired.

8. Refer to "Binding the Edges" on page 29 to cut 2¼"-wide bias strips for binding. Make a total of 385" of bias binding and sew it to the quilt-top edges.

9. Make a label and attach it to the back of the quilt.

# Alternative Color Scheme

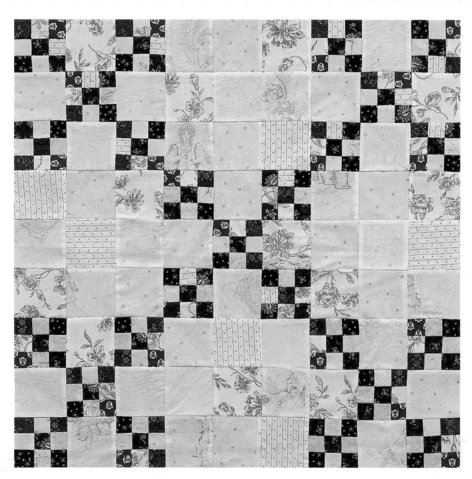

**Double Nine Patch** by Nancy J. Martin, Kingston, Washington, 2005.

Finished quilt size: 27" x 27"

Setting: 9 blocks set 3 across and 3 down,
alternating the Double Nine Patch and Nine Patch blocks

# Chinese Puzzle

By Nancy J. Martin and Cleo Nollette, Woodinville, Washington, 2004.

Quilted by Anna Stutzman, Mount Victory, Ohio.

Finished quilt size: 50" x 52½"

Finished block size: 10" x 10"

Setting: 7 blocks offset with various
setting pieces to create diagonal links;
2½"-wide pieced inner border; 5"-wide outer border

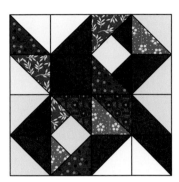

Chinese Puzzle

# MATERIALS

*Yardage is based on 42"-wide fabric.*

9 fat quarters of assorted beige or light cream prints for blocks, setting pieces, and pieced inner border

1⅝ yards of Asian-motif print for outer border and binding

7 fat eighths of assorted red or rust prints for blocks

3 yards of fabric for backing

Batting and thread to finish

Bias Square ruler to cut bias squares

# CUTTING

*All measurements include ¼"-wide seam allowances.*

**From the assorted beige or light cream prints, cut a *total* of:**

9 squares, 9" x 9"

14 squares, 2¼" x 2¼"

5 rectangles, 5½" x 10½" (setting piece 1)

2 rectangles, 5½" x 8" (setting piece 2)

1 rectangle, 8" x 10½" (setting piece 3)

3 squares, 5½" x 5½" (setting piece 4)

4 rectangles, 3" x 8" (setting piece 5)

1 rectangle, 3" x 5½" (setting piece 6)

8 squares, 3" x 3" (setting piece 7)

9 squares, 3" x 3"

3 rectangles, 3" x 5½"

9 strips, 3" x 8"

5 strips, 3" x 10½"

**From the assorted red or rust prints, cut a *total* of:**

13 squares, 9" x 9"

7 squares, 3¾" x 3¾"; cut each square in half twice diagonally to yield 28 triangles

14 squares, 3⅜" x 3⅜"; cut each square in half once diagonally to yield 28 triangles

**From the Asian-motif print, cut:**

5 strips, 5¼" x 42" (If your fabric is less than 40½" wide after preshrinking, you will need to cut an additional strip.)

# INSTRUCTIONS

1. Pair each 9" beige or cream square with a 9" red or rust square, right sides up. Referring to "Basic Bias Square Technique" on page 16, cut and piece 2¾"-wide strips, and then cut 70 bias squares, 3" x 3".

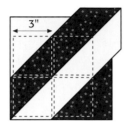

Cut 70.

2. Group the remaining 9" red or rust squares into two pairs. Repeat step 1 to cut 14 bias squares, 3" x 3".

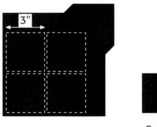

Cut 14.

3. Join one 2¼" beige or cream square, two small red or rust triangles, and two large red or rust triangles as shown. Make 14 units.

Make 14.

4. Join five bias squares from step 1, one bias square from step 2, and one unit from step 3 as shown. Make 14 units.

Make 14.

5. Join two units as shown to make a Chinese Puzzle block. Make five. The remaining units will be joined into blocks when the quilt sections are assembled.

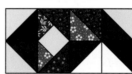

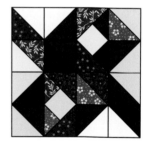

Make 5.

6. Stitch the completed blocks, the remaining block units, and the setting pieces into sections as shown.

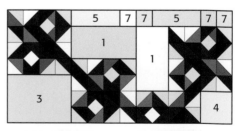

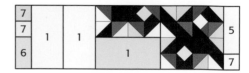

7. Join the sections to form the quilt top.

8. Piece the remaining beige or cream squares and rectangles together as shown to make the four border strips.

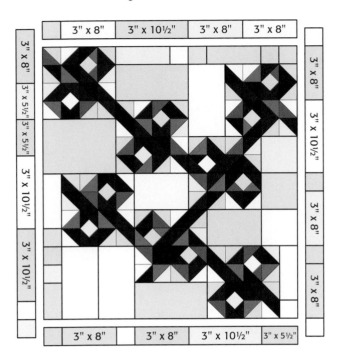

9. Refer to "Borders with Straight-Cut Corners" on page 23 to stitch the pieced borders to the quilt top. Repeat with the 5¼"-wide outer border strips.

   **Note:** Due to the Asian print's directional nature, I added the top and bottom borders first to best utilize the fabric and match the pattern.

10. Mark the quilt top with the design of your choice. Layer with batting and backing; baste. Hand or machine quilt as desired.

11. Refer to "Binding the Edges" on page 29 to cut 2¼"-wide bias strips for binding. Make a total of 212" of bias binding and sew it to the quilt-top edges.

12. Make a label and attach it to the back of the quilt.

## Alternative Color Scheme

**Chinese Puzzle** by Nancy J. Martin, Woodinville, Washington, 2003. Quilted by Anna Stutzman, Mount Victory, Ohio. Owned by Ursula Reikes.

Finished quilt size: 40" x 58½"

Setting: 10 blocks offset with various setting pieces to create diagonal links; 3"-wide outer border

# Nancy's Fancy

By Nancy J. Martin and Cleo Nollette, Kingston, Washington, 2004.
Quilted by Clara M. Yoder, Fredericksburg, Ohio.

Finished quilt size: 62" x 62"

Finished block size: 16" x 16"

Setting: 9 blocks set 3 across and 3 down;
1"-wide inner border; 6"-wide outer border

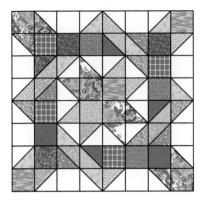

Nancy's Fancy

# MATERIALS

*Yardage is based on 42"-wide fabric.*

2¼ yards of floral print for blocks and outer border

8 fat quarters of assorted light fabrics for block background

8 fat quarters of assorted blue fabrics for blocks

6 fat quarters of assorted pink fabrics for blocks

½ yard of blue print for inner border

3⅝ yards of fabric for backing

⅞ yard of fabric for binding

Batting and thread to finish

Bias Square ruler to cut bias squares

# CUTTING

*All measurements include ¼"-wide seam allowances.*

**From *each* of the 8 light fat quarters, cut:**

4 squares, 8" x 8" (32 total)

9 squares, 2½" x 2½" (72 total)

**From *each* of the 8 blue fat quarters, cut:**

4 squares, 8" x 8" (32 total)

5 squares, 2½" x 2½" (40 total); you will use 36 and have 4 left over

**From *each* of the 6 pink fat quarters, cut:**

1 square, 8" x 8"; cut 1 extra square from 3 fabrics (9 total)

18 squares, 2½" x 2½" (108 total)

**From the blue print for inner border, cut:**

6 strips, 1½" x 42"

**From the floral print, cut:**

2 strips, 6¼" x 64", along the lengthwise grain

2 strips, 6¼" x 53", along the lengthwise grain

9 squares, 8" x 8"

36 squares, 2½" x 2½"

# INSTRUCTIONS

1. Pair 23 light 8" squares with blue 8" squares, right sides up. Referring to "Basic Bias Square Technique" on page 16, cut and piece 2½"-wide strips, and then cut 180 bias squares, 2½" x 2½".

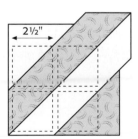

Cut 180.

2. Repeat step 1 to pair the pink 8" squares with the remaining blue 8" squares, and the floral 8" squares with the remaining light 8" squares. Cut 72 bias squares, 2½" x 2½", from *each* combination.

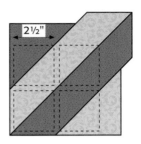

Cut 72.

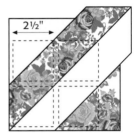

Cut 72.

3. Arrange the bias squares and 2½" squares into four rows as shown. Join the pieces in each row and then join the rows to make a half block. Make 18.

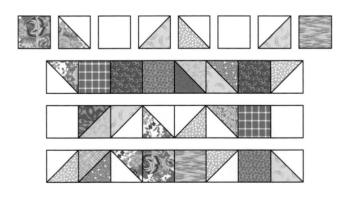

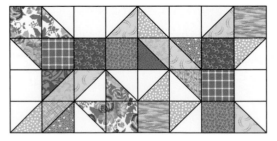

Make 18.

4. Join two block halves, flipping one as shown, to make a complete block. Make nine.

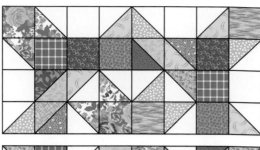

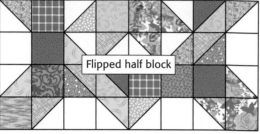

Flipped half block

Make 9.

5. Arrange and sew the blocks into three horizontal rows of three blocks each. Join the rows to form the quilt top.

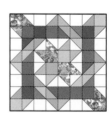
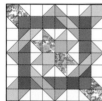
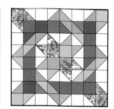

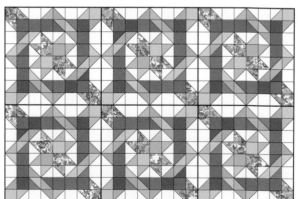

6. Refer to "Borders with Straight-Cut Corners" on page 23 to add the 1½"-wide inner border strips to the quilt top. Measure the quilt top for the outer borders. Trim the 6¼"-wide outer border strips to the exact lengths needed and attach them to the quilt top in the same manner as the inner border.

7. Mark the quilt top with the design of your choice. Layer with batting and backing; baste. Hand or machine quilt as desired.

8. Refer to "Binding the Edges" on page 29 to cut 2¼"-wide bias strips for binding. Make a total of 255" of bias binding and sew it to the quilt-top edges.

9. Make a label and attach it to the back of the quilt.

# Alternative Color Scheme

**Nancy's Fancy** by Cleo Nollette, Seattle, Washington, 2004.
Finished quilt size: 32" x 32"
Setting: 4 blocks set 2 across and 2 down

# House of Friendship

By Nancy J. Martin, Woodinville, Washington, 1994.

Quilted by Hazel Montague, Bellingham, Washington.

Finished quilt size: 76" x 91"

Finished block size: 15" x 15"

Setting: 20 blocks with frame and corner squares
set 4 across and 5 down; 8"-wide border

House of Friendship

**Design Note:** This quilt uses the fabric-recipe
approach for scrap quilts. Four major colors—red,
green, navy, and assorted lights—are used for
various house parts. None of the houses uses
identical fabric combinations.

## MATERIALS

*Yardage is based on 42"-wide fabric.*

16 fat quarters of assorted light fabrics for
background, windows, and framing

10 fat quarters of assorted red fabrics for
chimneys, houses, and framing

10 fat quarters of assorted navy fabrics for houses
and framing

10 fat quarters of assorted green fabrics for roofs
and framing

2½ yards of navy print for border

1 yard of fabric for binding

5¾ yards of fabric for backing

Batting and thread to finish

## CUTTING

*All measurements include ¼"-wide seam allowances.
Templates are on pages 94 and 95.*

**From *each* of the 10 red fat quarters, cut:**

4 squares, 2½" x 2½", for chimneys (40 total)

8 rectangles, 1½" x 4½", for left side of house
(80 total)

2 of template C (20 total)

2 strips, 2" x 12½", for framing (20 total)

2 squares, 2" x 2", for framing corner squares
(20 total)

**From *each* of the 10 navy fat quarters, cut:**

6 rectangles, 1½" x 3½", for right side of house
(60 total)

4 rectangles, 1½" x 7½", for right side of house
(40 total)

2 rectangles, 2" x 12½", for framing (20 total)

2 squares, 2" x 2", for framing corner squares
(20 total)

**From *each* of the 10 green fat quarters, cut:**

2 of template A (20 total)

2 strips, 2" x 12½", for framing (20 total)

2 squares, 2" x 2", for framing corner squares
(20 total)

**From the assorted light fabrics, cut a total of:**

*For each piece marked with an asterisk (\*), cut one
piece from any of the assorted light fabrics, and then
cut one piece from that same fabric for each of the
other pieces marked with an asterisk, with the
exception of the 2½" squares of which you will cut
two pieces from the same fabric. Repeat until you have
the necessary amount of pieces. Do the same with the
pieces marked with two asterisks (\*\*) and three
asterisks (\*\*\*).*

20 of template D for background\*

20 of template D reversed for background\*

20 of template B for background\*\*

20 rectangles, 2½" x 4½", for background\*

40 squares, 2½" x 2½", for background\*

20 rectangles, 1½" x 6½", for background**

20 rectangles, 1½" x 7½", for background**

20 rectangles, 2½" x 4½", for large window***

20 rectangles, 2½" x 3½", for small windows**

20 rectangles, 2" x 12½", for framing

20 squares, 2" x 2", for framing corner squares

**From the navy print, cut:**
4 strips, 8¼" x 78", along the lengthwise grain

# INSTRUCTIONS

1. Using matching light pieces, join one *each* of pieces A, B, C, D, and D reversed; two 2½" light squares; two 2½" red squares; and one 2½" x 4½" light rectangle as shown to make the top half of the house. Press as desired.

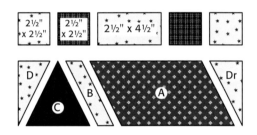

2. Using pieces from the same light fabric that you used in step 1, join one 1½" x 7½" light rectangle, two 1½" x 7½" navy rectangles, three 1½" x 3½" navy rectangles, and two 2½" x 3½" light rectangles as shown to construct the right side of each house. To make the left side of each house, join four 1½" x 4½" red rectangles, one 2½" x 4½" light rectangle, and one 1½" x 6½" light rectangle as shown. Stitch the left and right sides of the house together to make the bottom half of the house. Press as desired.

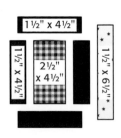
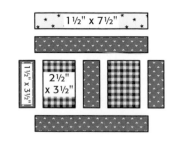

3. Sew the top and bottom halves together. Press the seam toward the bottom half.

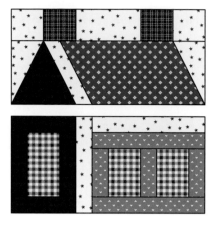

4. Repeat steps 1–3 to make a total of 20 house units.

5. Stitch the 2" x 12½" rectangles and the 2" squares to the house units as shown to complete the blocks. Press the seams toward the framing rectangles.

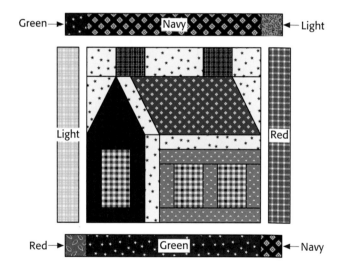

6. Arrange the blocks in five horizontal rows of four blocks each. Sew the blocks in each row together. Press seams in opposite directions from row to row. Sew the rows together.

7. Refer to "Borders with Straight-Cut Corners" on page 23 to measure the quilt top for borders. Trim the 8¼"-wide border strips to the exact lengths needed and attach them to the quilt top.

8. Mark the quilt top with the design of your choice. Layer with batting and backing; baste. Hand or machine quilt as desired.

9. Refer to "Binding the Edges" on page 29 to cut 2¼"-wide bias strips for binding. Make a total of 346" of bias binding and sew it to the quilt-top edges.

10. Make a label and attach it to the back of the quilt.

## Alternative Color Scheme

**Dream House** by Nancy J. Martin, Woodinville, Washington, 1999.

Quilted by Elsie Mast, Charm, Ohio.

Finished quilt size: 60" x 60"

Setting: 9 blocks with frame and corner squares set 3 across and 3 down; 7½"-wide border

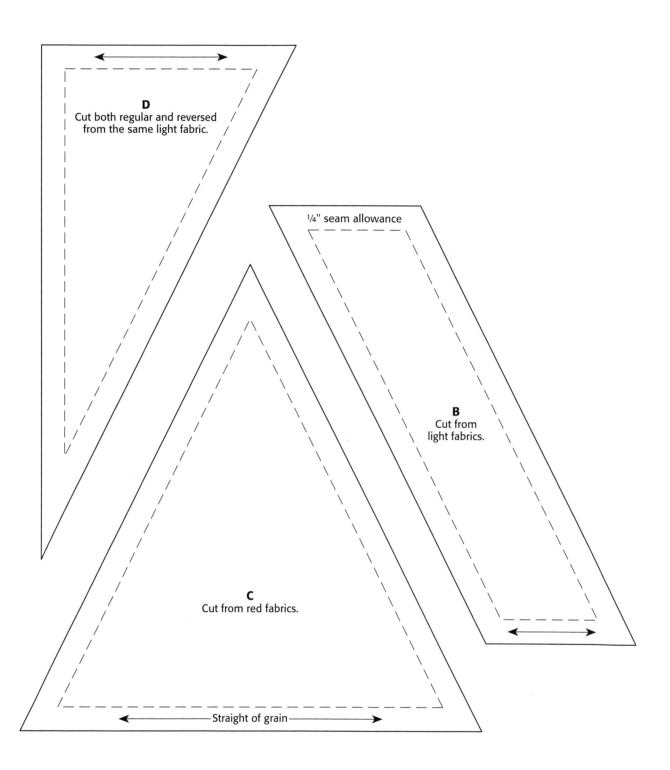

**D**
Cut both regular and reversed
from the same light fabric.

¼" seam allowance

**B**
Cut from
light fabrics.

**C**
Cut from red fabrics.

Straight of grain

Straight of grain

**A**
Cut from green fabrics.

¼" seam allowance

# Corner Star

By Nancy J. Martin and Cleo Nollette, Kingston, Washington, 2004.
Quilted by Treva Mast, Kenton, Ohio.

Finished quilt size: 63½" x 63½"

Finished block size: 17" x 17"

Setting: 9 blocks set 3 across and 3 down;
6¼"-wide pieced border

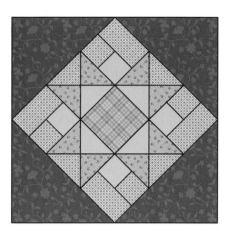

Corner Star

**Design Note:** Preplan your blocks by selecting the fabrics to be used in each one. You will need one pink print, one light green print, and two medium green prints. The plaid fabric is used for the center of each block.

# MATERIALS

*Yardage is based on 42"-wide fabric.*

¾ yard *each* of 6 medium green prints for blocks and pieced border

½ yard *each* of 6 light green prints for blocks and pieced border

4 fat quarters of assorted light pink prints for blocks and pieced border

1 fat quarter of plaid fabric for blocks and pieced border

4 yards of fabric for backing

⅞ yard of fabric for binding

Batting and thread to finish

# CUTTING

*All measurements include ¼"-wide seam allowances.*

**From one light green print, cut:**
*Repeat the following cutting instructions a total of 9 times.*

4 squares, 2½" x 2½"

4 rectangles, 2½" x 4½"

1 square, 5¼" x 5¼"; cut the square in half twice diagonally to yield 4 triangles

**From one medium green print, cut:**
*Repeat the following cutting instructions a total of 9 times.*

1 square, 5¼" x 5¼"; cut the square in half twice diagonally to yield 4 triangles

4 squares, 2½" x 2½"

**From a different medium green print, cut:**
*Repeat the following cutting instructions a total of 9 times.*

2 squares, 9⅜" x 9⅜"; cut each square in half once diagonally to yield 4 triangles

**From one pink print, cut:**
*Repeat the following cutting instructions a total of 9 times.*

2 squares, 5¼" x 5¼"; cut each square in half twice diagonally to yield 8 triangles

**From the plaid fabric, cut:**
9 squares, 4½" x 4½", for block centers

**From the remainder of *each* of the pink prints, cut:**
1 square, 3½" x 3½" (4 total)

**From the remainder of the plaid, light green, and medium green fabrics, cut a *total* of:**
12 strips, 3½" x 42"

4 rectangles, 3½" x 6½"

4 squares, 3½" x 3½"

# INSTRUCTIONS

1. Join one 2½" x 4½" light green rectangle, a matching 2½" light green square, and a 2½" medium green square as shown to make a block corner unit. Make four matching units.

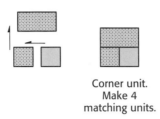

Corner unit.
Make 4
matching units.

2. Using the same light and medium green prints you used in step 1, join two matching pink triangles, one light green triangle, and one small medium-green triangle as shown to make a side unit. Make four matching units.

Side unit.
Make 4
matching units.

3. Join the four corner and side units and one 4½" plaid square as shown.

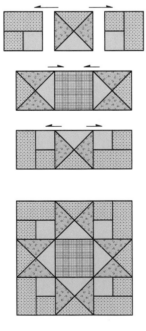

4. Stitch four matching large medium-green triangles to each star unit, joining opposite sides first to make the Corner Star block.

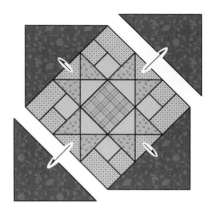

5. Repeat steps 1–4 to make nine blocks.

6. Arrange and sew the blocks into three rows of three blocks each. Join the rows.

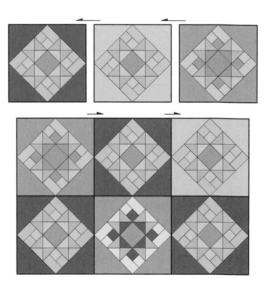

7. Join six 3½" x 42" strips together along the long edges. Make two strip sets. From the strip sets, cut 12 segments, 6½" wide.

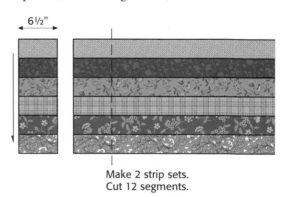

6½"

Make 2 strip sets.
Cut 12 segments.

8. Join three segments from step 7 end to end to make four border strips. Remove one piece from the end of each strip.

Make 4.

Remove one strip.

9. Join a 3½" x 6½" light green rectangle, a 3½" light green square, and a 3½" pink square as shown to make two variations of pieced corner squares. Make two of each variation.

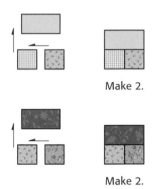

Make 2.

Make 2.

10. Join the pieced borders to the sides of the quilt top. Add a pieced corner square to each end of the remaining pieced borders as shown. Add these strips to the top and bottom edges of the quilt top.

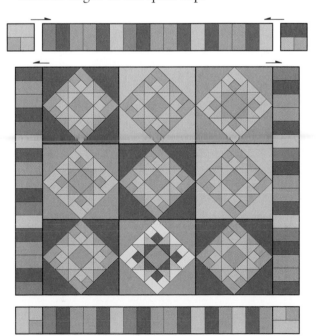

11. Mark the quilt top with the design of your choice. Layer with batting and backing; baste. Hand or machine quilt as desired.

12. Refer to "Binding the Edges" on page 29 to cut 2¼"-wide bias strips for binding. Make a total of 264" of bias binding and sew it to the quilt-top edges.

13. Make a label and attach it to the back of the quilt.

## Alternative Color Scheme

**Corner Star** by Nancy J. Martin, Woodinville, Washington, 1999.

Quilted by Fannie Yoder, Charm, Ohio.

Finished quilt size: 63½" x 63½"

Setting: 9 blocks set 3 across and 3 down; 6¼"-wide pieced border

# Scrappy Star

By Nancy J. Martin, Kingston, Washington, 2004.
Quilted by Lydia Troyer, Mount Victory, Ohio.

Finished quilt size: 60" x 60"

Finished block size: 12" x 12"

Setting: 16 blocks, set 4 across and 4 down;
1"-wide inner border; 5"-wide outer border

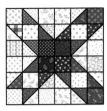 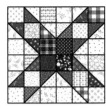 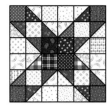

Scrappy Stars

## MATERIALS

*Yardage is based on 42"-wide fabric.*

3 yards *total* of assorted light fabrics for block
background

2¼ yards *total* of assorted blue fabrics for blocks

6 fat eighths of red fabric for blocks

1⅛ yards of blue fabric for outer border

⅜ yard of red fabric for inner border

3⅝ yards of fabric for backing

⅞ yard of fabric for binding

Batting and thread to finish

Bias Square ruler to cut bias squares

## CUTTING

*All measurements include ¼"-wide seam allowances.*

**From the assorted light fabrics, cut a *total* of:**
32 squares, 8" x 8"

220 squares, 2½" x 2½"

**From the assorted blue fabrics, cut a *total* of:**
32 squares, 8" x 8"

36 squares, 2½" x 2½"

**From the fat eighths of red fabric, cut a
*total* of:**
64 squares, 2½" x 2½"

**From the red fabric for inner border, cut:**
6 strips, 1½" x 42"

**From the blue fabric for outer border, cut:**
2 strips, 5¼" x 52", along the lengthwise grain

2 strips, 5¼" x 62", along the lengthwise grain

## INSTRUCTIONS

1. Pair each 8" light square with an 8" blue
   square, right sides up. Referring to "Basic
   Bias Square Technique" on page 16, cut and
   piece 2½"-wide strips, and then cut 256 bias
   squares, 2½" x 2½".

Cut 256.

2. Join red, blue, and light 2½" squares with
   bias squares as shown to make four corner
   blocks.

Corner block.
Make 4.

3. Join red, blue, and light 2½" squares with bias squares as shown to make eight edge blocks.

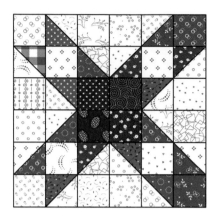

Edge block.
Make 8.

4. Join the remaining red, blue, and light 2½" squares with bias squares as shown to make four center blocks.

Center block.
Make 4.

5. Make the top and bottom rows of the quilt by joining two edge blocks between two corner blocks as shown.

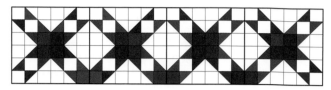

Make 2.

6. Make the two center rows by joining two center blocks between two edge blocks as shown.

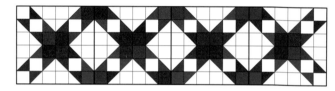

Make 2.

7. Join the rows as shown.

8. Refer to "Borders with Straight-Cut Corners" on page 23 to add the 1½"-wide inner border strips to the quilt top. Measure the quilt top for the outer borders. Trim the 5¼"-wide outer border strips to the exact lengths needed and attach them to the quilt top in the same manner as the inner border.

9. Mark the quilt top with the design of your choice. Layer with batting and backing; baste. Hand or machine quilt as desired.

10. Refer to "Binding the Edges" on page 29 to cut 2¼"-wide bias strips for binding. Make a total of 250" of bias binding and sew it to the quilt-top edges.

11. Make a label and attach it to the back of the quilt.

## Alternative Color Scheme

**Scrappy Star** by Nancy J. Martin, Woodinville, Washington, 1994.
Quilted by Donna Gundlach, Olympia, Washington.
Finished quilt size: 32" x 32"
Setting: 4 blocks set 2 across and 2 down; 1"-wide inner border; 3"-wide outer border

# C-Clamp

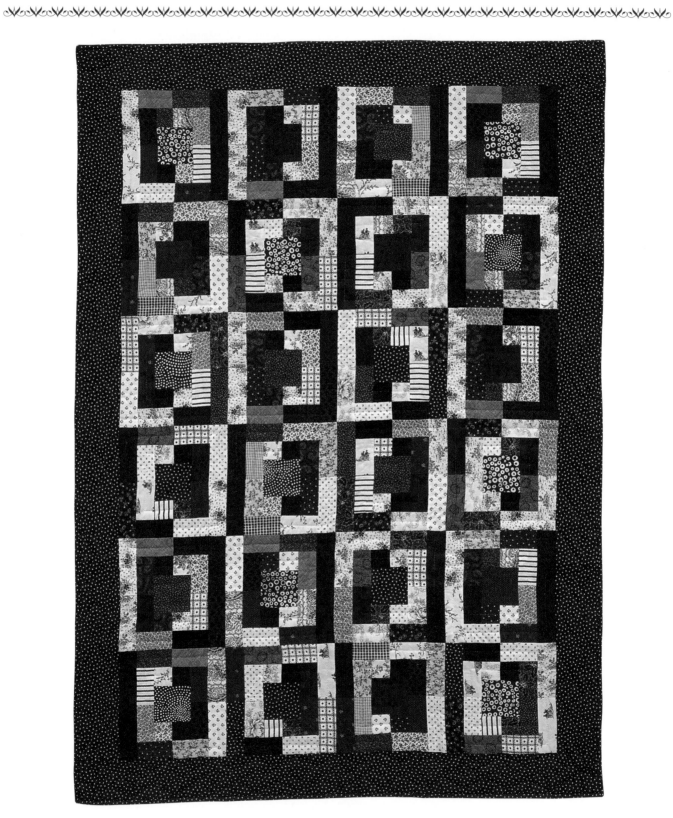

By Nancy J. Martin, Kingston, Washington, 2004.
Quilted by Emma Miller, Navarre, Ohio.

Finished quilt size: 44" x 62"

Finished block size: 9" x 9"

Setting: 24 blocks set 4 across and 6 down; 4"-wide border

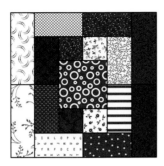

C-Clamp

## MATERIALS

*Yardage is based on 42"-wide fabric.*

10 fat quarters of assorted light prints for blocks

10 fat quarters of assorted red prints for blocks

⅞ yard of red print for border

2¾ yards of fabric for backing

⅞ yard of fabric for binding

Batting and thread to finish

## CUTTING

*All measurements include ¼"-wide seam allowances.*

**From the assorted red prints, cut a *total* of:**

24 squares, 3½" x 3½"

5 strips, 2" x 22"

11 strips, 3½" x 22"

6 strips, 5" x 22"

**From the assorted light prints, cut a *total* of:**

5 strips, 2" x 22"

11 strips, 3½" x 22"

6 strips, 5" x 22"

**From the red print for border, cut:**

2 strips, 4¼" x 56", along the lengthwise grain

2 strips, 4¼" x 46", along the lengthwise grain

## INSTRUCTIONS

1. Stitch a 2" x 22" light strip to one long edge of a 2" x 22" red strip to make a strip set. Make five. From the strip sets, cut 48 segments, 2" wide.

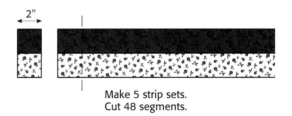

Make 5 strip sets.
Cut 48 segments.

2. Stitch a 3½" x 22" light strip to one long edge of a 3½" x 22" red strip to make a strip set. Make five. From the strip sets, cut 48 segments, 2" wide.

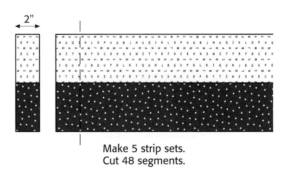

Make 5 strip sets.
Cut 48 segments.

3. Stitch a 3½" x 22" red strip to one long edge of a 3½" x 22" strip of a different red to make a strip set. Make three. From the strip sets, cut 24 segments, 2" wide. Repeat with the remaining 3½" x 22" light strips.

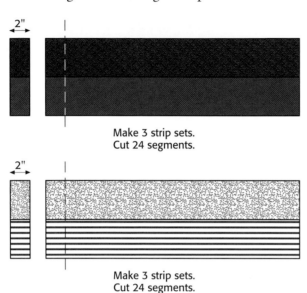

Make 3 strip sets.
Cut 24 segments.

Make 3 strip sets.
Cut 24 segments.

4. Stitch a 5" x 22" red strip to one long edge of a 5" x 22" strip of a different red to make a strip set. Make three. From the strip sets, cut 24 segments, 2" wide. Repeat with the 5" x 22" light strips.

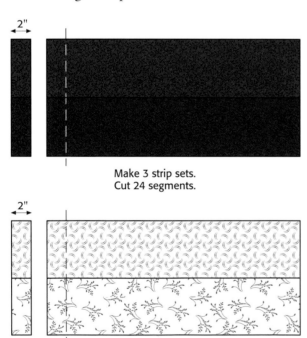

Make 3 strip sets.
Cut 24 segments.

Make 3 strip sets.
Cut 24 segments.

5. Stitch the segments together as shown to make a C-Clamp block. Make 24.

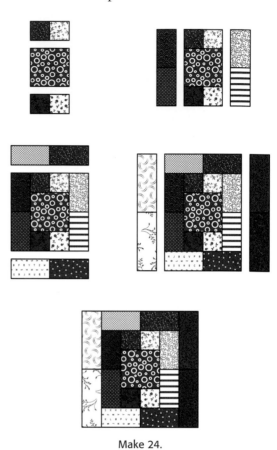

Make 24.

6. Arrange the blocks into six horizontal rows of four blocks each as shown, rotating the blocks from row to row to form the pattern. Sew the blocks in each row together. Sew the rows together to form the quilt top.

7. Refer to "Borders with Straight-Cut Corners" on page 23 to measure the quilt top for borders. Trim the 4¼"-wide border strips to the exact lengths needed and attach them to the quilt top.

8. Mark the quilt top with the design of your choice. Layer with batting and backing; baste. Hand or machine quilt as desired.

9. Refer to "Binding the Edges" on page 29 to cut 2¼"-wide bias strips for binding. Make a total of 220" of bias binding and sew it to the quilt-top edges.

10. Make a label and attach it to the back of the quilt.

## Alternative Color Scheme

**C-Clamp** by Cleo Nollette, Seattle, Washington, 2004.

Finished quilt size: 18" x 18"

Setting: 4 blocks set 2 across and down

# French Medallion

**Blue Fleur Medallion** by Nancy J. Martin, Woodinville, Washington, 2004.
Quilted by Clara Yoder, Fredericksburg, Ohio.

Finished quilt size: 64" x 64"

Finished medallion size: 24" x 24"

Setting: 24" framed medallion; 2"-wide pieced
first border; 2"-wide second border; 4"-wide pieced third
border; 4"-wide pieced fourth border;
8"-wide outer border

## MATERIALS

*Yardage is based on 42"-wide fabric.*

2⅛ yards of blue fabric for outer border and
binding

7 fat quarters of assorted light fabrics for background and appliqués

7 fat quarters of assorted dark blue fabrics for
background and appliqués

¾ yard of fabric for center medallion background
or 24½" x 24½" printed panel*

⅜ yard of floral print for second border

¼ yard of blue-and-white check fabric for flower
stems

Scraps of red for appliqués

4 yards of fabric for backing

4 different small red buttons for flower centers

Batting and thread to finish

Bias Square ruler to cut bias squares

¼"-wide bias bar or Celtic bar for making stems

*\*I used a printed scarf as the background for the
center appliqué.*

## CUTTING

*All measurements include ¼"-wide seam allowances*

**From the center medallion fabric, cut:**
1 square, 24½" x 24½"

**From *each* of the 7 light fat quarters, cut:**
2 squares, 5¼" x 5¼" (14 total); cut each square
in half twice diagonally to yield 56 triangles

1 square, 9¼" x 9¼" (7 total); cut each square in
half twice diagonally to yield 28 triangles. You
will use 20 and have 8 left over.

**From *each* of the 7 dark blue fat quarters, cut:**
5 squares, 5¼" x 5¼" (35 total); cut each square
in half twice diagonally to yield 140 triangles

1 square, 9¼" x 9¼" (7 total); cut each square in
half twice diagonally to yield 28 triangles. You
will use 24 and have 4 left over.

**From the floral print, cut:**
4 strips, 2½" x 42"

**From the blue fabric for outer border, cut:**
2 strips, 8¼" x 50", along the lengthwise grain
2 strips, 8¼" x 67", along the lengthwise grain

## INSTRUCTIONS

1. Refer to "Appliqué" on page 21 to cut the
   appliqué shapes on page 111 from the
   appropriate fabrics as indicated on the
   patterns. Refer to "Bias Stems" on page 22
   to cut the blue check fabric into ¾"-wide bias
   strips and make bias tubes for the stems. Cut
   the bias tubes to the desired lengths for the
   stems. Appliqué the pieces to the background
   as shown.

Appliqué placement

2. Join seven small dark blue background triangles and six small light background triangles as shown to make a strip for the first border. Make four.

3. Join the pieced border strips to the center medallion, positioning the light triangles next to the medallion. Miter the corners, referring to "Borders with Mitered Corners" on page 24.

4. Join the floral strips to the quilt top for the second border, referring to "Borders with Straight-Cut Corners" on page 23.

5. Join one small light triangle and three small dark blue triangles as shown to make unit 1. Make 32. Join four small dark blue triangles in the same manner to make unit 2. Make four.

Unit 1.
Make 32.

Unit 2.
Make 4.

6. Stitch eight unit 1 squares together as shown to make a third border strip. Make four.

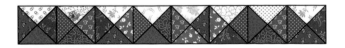

7. Join a border strip to each side of the quilt top, positioning the light triangles next to the floral border.

8. Stitch a unit 2 square to the ends of the remaining two border strips. Stitch these strips to the top and bottom of the quilt top, positioning the light triangles next to the floral border.

9. Refer to step 2 to join six large dark blue triangles and five large light triangles to make four pieced fourth border strips.

10. Join the pieced border strips to the quilt top, mitering the corners.

11. Refer to "Borders with Straight-Cut Corners" on page 23 to measure the quilt top for the outer borders. Trim the 8¼"-wide blue strips to the exact lengths needed and attach them to the quilt top.

12. Mark the quilt top with the design of your choice. Layer with batting and backing; baste. Hand or machine quilt as desired. Add buttons to morning glory centers after quilting is complete.

13. Refer to "Binding the Edges" on page 29 to cut 2¼"-wide bias strips for binding. Make a total of 260" of bias binding and sew it to the quilt-top edges.

14. Make a label and attach it to the back of the quilt.

# Alternative Color Scheme

**Pretty in Pink** by Nancy J. Martin, Kingston, Washington, 2005.

Finished quilt size: 48" x 48"
Setting: 24" square; 2"-wide pieced first border; 2"-wide second border; 4"-wide pieced third border; 4"-wide outer border

**Morning glory flower base**
Cut 4 from dark blue fabrics.

**Basket rim**
Cut 1 from light fabric.

**Tulip**
Cut 8 from red fabrics.

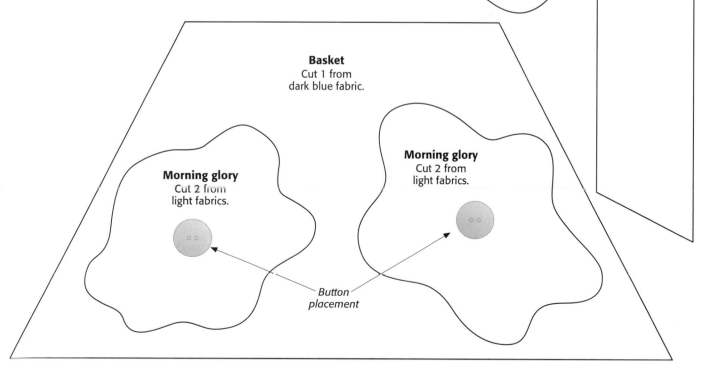

**Basket**
Cut 1 from dark blue fabric.

**Morning glory**
Cut 2 from light fabrics.

**Morning glory**
Cut 2 from light fabrics.

*Button placement*

# About the Author

Nancy J. Martin is a talented teacher and quiltmaker who has written more than 40 books on quiltmaking. An innovator in the quilting industry, she introduced the Bias Square cutting ruler to quilters everywhere. Nancy was the 2002 recipient of the prestigious Silver Star Award. This recognition comes from Quilts, Inc., sponsor of the largest biannual trade show in the quilting industry, International Quilt Market and Festival. The award is presented annually to an individual whose artistry, enthusiasm, and promotion of quilting has made a lasting impact on the quilting industry and community.

Along with having more than 25 years of teaching experience and several bestselling titles to her credit, Nancy is the founder and president of Martingale & Company, the publisher of America's Best-Loved Quilt Books®. She and her husband, Dan, enjoy living in the Pacific Northwest.